RUNNING YOUR BEST RACE
Programs for Improving Speed and Distance

Joe Henderson

ωcb

Wm. C. Brown Publishers
Dubuque, Iowa

Books by Joe Henderson

The Long Run Solution (1976)
Jog, Run, Race (1977)
Run Farther, Run Faster (1979)
The Running Revolution (1980)
Running, A to Z (1982)
Running for Fitness, for Sport,
and for Life (1984)
Running Your Best Race (1984)

Photography
Bob Coyle
34, 66, 72, 120
Dave Madison—
cover photo, 2, 8, 14, 22, 28, 38, 50, 56, 78, 90, 96, 102,
109, 114, 128, 134, 140, 146, 152, 158, 164, 170, 174, 180
Jim Schaffer
44, 48

Illustrations
All drawings by Don Person,
reprinted from *Running for Fitness, for Sport, and for Life*
(Wm. C. Brown Publishers, 1984)

Paper
Library of Congress Catalog Card Number: 84–72143
ISBN 0–697–00458–9

Comb-Apple II Version
Library of Congress Catalog Card Number: 84–072145
ISBN 0–697–00459–7

Comb-IBM PC Version
Library of Congress Catalog Card Number: 84–072144
ISBN 0–697–00460–0

Printed in the United States of America

Dedication

For Fred Wilt, Arthur Newton, Ernst van Aaken, Arthur Lydiard and Bill Bowerman: the men whose writings taught me how to run my best races; the giants on whose shoulders I now stand as a writer.

Contents

Tables and Figures

Preface

Public speaking once topped my all-time list of painful acts. Facing crowds and letting my words reach them without editing used to terrify me. I dreaded the speech for days in advance, and after presenting it, needed weeks to work up the courage to speak again.

I list that trauma in the past tense, because I'm past being tense. I feel as relaxed on stage now as I do talking away the miles of a Sunday morning run or replaying a race over a meal with friends. The pain of speech-making vanished when I quit *speaking to* crowds of people and began *talking with* persons in those audiences.

After introductions, I now say, "That's enough about me. We're here tonight to talk about you and your interests. Any questions?"

This opening startles the audience into silence. These people came expecting to be lectured in normal running-clinic fashion for the next hour, and here the speaker is asking to be told what to say. No one speaks.

I ask who is in the crowd by calling for a show of hands to indicate running experience and interests. A second request for questions yields none.

"Come on," I plead. "You wouldn't be here if you didn't want to learn ways to run farther and faster, or to make your running healthier and happier. Who'll be first? Don't worry about asking something silly. The only foolish question is the one not asked."

As I look from face to face, eyes turn downward. No hand goes up.

"That's okay. I'll let you off the hook for a while by guessing your questions. Certain ones come up whenever runners meet. For instance, . . ."

That lead-in ploy seldom fails to tap a well of curiosity, and for the next hour or more, I respond to questions and comments from the floor. These runners seem to like the dialogue format as much as I do.

They teach me as much as I teach them. I learn from this two-way talk what runners really want to know, and how well the neat packages of advice in articles and books really work when the theories are put to a road test.

In the bad old days of speaking, my lectures parroted advice from my articles and earlier books. Now I've compiled a book along the lines of these public conversations. I introduce myself, and ask you to introduce yourself to me. Then I anticipate the questions that most concern you. Together, we arrive at solutions to your problems.

Introducing me: I have run for more than twenty-five years, raced more than 600 times at distances as short as 100 yards and as long as 100 miles. My personal mile record is 4:18, my 10-K 33:45, my marathon 2:49:48.

Those times came long ago and far away. All serious racing is behind me, and I run (and occasionally still race) without specific goals. I'm a Stage Three runner who runs for the fun of running.

Earlier, however, I evolved through the first two stages: exercising to establish basic fitness, and then training for higher speeds and longer distances. An already fit fourteen-year-old, I was a Stage One only a few weeks. Racing improvement, however, lasted a full 10 years, until I didn't need it any more to keep going. Stage Three, the recreational phase now in its sixteenth year, appears endless.

My story is not unique. My evolutionary course is similar to one that most runners follow.

Introducing you: I'm assuming a lot about you. You are a second-stage runner. You're long past jogging for fitness, but not yet ready to settle down to fun-running. Running in races "just to finish" no longer satisfies you, and you're not yet ready to treat races as social events. You want to learn how you can race faster and farther.

You don't place yourself among the competitive elite. You're concerned with improving your own times, not with beating other runners. You aren't interested in either the sprints or the ultradistances. You feel most at home in road races five kilometers to half-marathon, although you make rare forays down to the mile and up to the marathon.

You seek short-term gains in time and distance, but not at the expense of long-term health and enjoyment. You take your running seriously for the hour a day that you devote to it, but you don't let it become a second job.

I know who you are and where you want to go. I've been there.

Introducing the book: This is a do-it-yourself manual for racers. It is not a primer on establishing first-stage fitness; nor is it a philosophical roadmap for Stage Three runners. Two of my earlier books, *Running: The First Steps* and *Running: A to Z,* and dozens of volumes from other authors cover the territory on both sides of racing.

This isn't *my* book; it is *ours*. I provide a skeleton of advice, then leave to you the task of adding flesh and blood to those bare bones. I'm not your coach—only your advisor. I advise you on how to coach yourself, assess your abilities and ambitions, write your training schedules, and plan and execute your races.

The advice is mine; the work to implement it and then the better times ahead are yours. My past and your future come together on the pages that follow.

Joe Henderson
Eugene, Oregon
July 1984

Prologue

Two somebodies with well-known names, one male and one female, lead their divisions at each big race. We watch them on television that day and read about them in the newspapers the next morning as if they were the only people running.

I don't begrudge these two runners their moments of glory. And since I'm in the news business myself, I know that the headlines and the choice video footage come from the front of the pack.

But as a runner who has been a small part of hundreds of big road races, and has never finished first, I also know how important the rest of the story is. It's the story you'll never read about in a newspaper or see as anything more than an oozing, multicolored mass when the TV cameras briefly shift their focus off the front-runners for a crowd shot from above.

This story really is thousands of individual stories, each one meaning much more to its author than any developments on the road up ahead. Runners have their own work to do, their own races to run, their own private victories to celebrate when their run is done.

While handing out awards at a race in Tacoma, Washington, I noted that most of the runners hadn't won any prizes they could place on a mantle or tack onto a bulletin board. Then I added, "You all are carrying home something of greater value."

I asked those who had run their first race to stand, then those who had run farther than ever before, finally those who had run their fastest at this distance. More than half of the crowd stood, and the people still seated applauded.

"Will those who think they failed or lost today please hold up your hands?" I said. No one did. This may only have shown reluctance to admit failure, but I doubt it.

"This," I said, "is what the running revolution is all about: everyone feeling like a winner and wanting to keep on winning. To participate is to win. To improve yourself is to win bigger, and the only way to lose is to stop."

This running revolution is not one of numbers. Sure, we've all heard that 20 or 25 or 30 million Americans run (depending upon which poll you believe, and how strictly you define running and runners), and more than a million of them race long distances on the roads.

The numbers boom is an effect of the running revolution, not a cause. Before the sport could enjoy its incredible growth spurt (which continues, by the way—much to the dismay of critics who've been predicting the decline and fall of running for years), we had to pass through a revolution of *attitudes*. Mainly, "losers" had to decide they could win.

I'm a reformed loser. When I began running in the 1950s, I believed what I know now to be the Three Great Lies of Sport: (1) There can be no gain without pain; (2) there can be but one winner; (3) there can be no running without success in racing.

To swallow the first lie is to believe that running must hurt all the time; that it is always serious, grinding work; that a strong mind must beat a reluctant body into shape; that this unpleasantness is tolerated only for the results it gives.

The second lie implies that second place means nothing; defeat is a step removed from death; only the person who finishes first is allowed to be happy, and then only for as long as he or she stays on top.

Lie three says that anyone whose painful work isn't paying off with first-place finishes or the reasonable prospect of achieving them should get out of the sport; be a spectator for the fastest and fittest people who survive this brutal natural-selection process.

When the sport still lived by these lies, as most other sports still do, not many people ran. If a group of high school or college runners had been asked 10 or 20 years ago, "When do you plan to quit?" most of them would have answered, "As soon as I graduate," or, "As soon as I stop improving." Many of them secretly hoped for a serious injury that would let them leave this dreary business sooner, yet with honor.

Ask today's runners the same question about when they intend to stop, and most of them will answer without hesitation, "Never!" They dread most an injury that might end their running.

This attitude shows how dramatically our ideas on racing and training have changed during the running revolution. The sport has evolved from painful to pleasurable, runners from being hero-worshippers to their own heroes, racing from a be-all to a by-product.

We have learned that this sport is too good to hurt all the time, too good to belong only to the people who race fastest, too good to leave behind when our own racing times stop improving.

We are free now to run with little pain, but who is to say we aren't gaining? We are free to finish far behind the leaders in races, but no one can call us anything but winners. We who run for fun want to run forever, and that is the greatest victory of all.

TRAINING

CHAPTER ONE

The Foundation

Simple as 1-2-3

The nicest compliment anyone can give me as a writer is to say that I made sense. Someone who reads or hears my words can't flatter me more than by saying, "You made everything so clear and simple." The reader doesn't need to say the delivery was eloquent or that he or she agreed with the messages—only that he or she understood. If a talk or article simplifies the complex, it is successful. If it complicates the simple, it is a failure.

Training for racing is really a very simple matter. Hundreds of books have been written about this subject, but they can be condensed to six essential words: *long enough, fast enough, easy enough.*

Essentially, training combines the elements of distance, speed and recovery into a schedule that matches one's running abilities and ambitions. These are the basic ingredients, the staples of a runner's diet, which will be combined later into palatable recipes.

The first two items are "tests"—a blanket term covering long runs, speedwork, and time trials. These are dress rehearsals for racing. By necessity, the tests are hard work. They prepare you for the even harder work of racing.

Long tests mimic the distance of the race, but at a slower pace. Fast tests prepare you for the race's full speed, but cover only part of its distance. You combine full distance with full speed only in the race itself, where it counts. Testing will be discussed more thoroughly in Part Two.

We examine the third ingredient—recovery—first, since it constitutes the bulk of any well-rounded training diet. For each race and race-like test, plan about ten times as much recovery running. Hard running tears you down, while easier running builds you back up. The tearing down occurs quickly; repairing takes much longer.

These recovery runs are neither very long nor very fast, and they should never be overly demanding. They are meant to restore energy and enthusiasm drained away by hard work.

We visit the extremes of distance and speed occasionally for challenge and excitement. But the spaces between races and tests are where we live.

Managing Stress

Athletic training is essentially an exercise in balancing stress loads. Apply the proper types of stresses in the proper amounts, and you become a fitter athlete. Understress, and you don't improve. Overstress, and your performance and perhaps even your health suffer.

Forbes Carlile translated Dr. Hans Selye's theories of stress management into athletic terms. Carlile, an Australian, gained attention in the 1960s and 70s as a coach of swimmers, including Olympic champion Shane Gould. But he entered the sports world as a long-distance runner, then graduated to studying the entire field of exercise physiology and athletic training.

Carlile developed ten guidelines applying to all types of athletic training and to all athletes. Physiologists and coaches now generally agree on a set of principles that read very much like Carlile's original list. Working within these physical laws should lead to the desired training effects.

1. **Principle of stress:**
   Stress, in manageable amounts, is the stimulus that provokes a training response. The stress must be regular and strong enough to stimulate adaptation. But it should not occur in such heavy and frequent doses that it overwhelms the adaptation system, causing a breakdown.

   Running itself is only one of many stresses acting on a runner. Others include faulty diet, psychic unrest, and environmental insults such as extreme heat and cold. Runners must consider the stress burden as a whole and then adapt their workloads to it.

2. **Principle of overload:**
   "Overload" is not the same as "overwork." Overloading is selective stressing: enough to stimulate the desired response without producing exhaustion.

Forbes Carlile said, "The training load must be severe, and must be applied frequently enough and with sufficient intensity to cause the body to adapt maximally to a particular activity." But he added, "It is at the same time true that sustained all-out efforts in training or in races should be made only sparingly."

This is what renowned coach Arthur Lydiard from New Zealand meant by his now-famous adage: "Train, don't strain." No results can come without training, yet straining too hard and too often is self-defeating. Lydiard asserted that training should be an everyday, year-round activity, but no more than ten percent of a runner's efforts should be race-like.

3. **Principle of specificity:**

Even though all training cannot be exactly like racing, it must be a close approximation. The system adapts to the specific exercise it is given. Walk, and you become fit for walking; bicycle, and you become a better biker; run, and you get into shape for running. There is little carry-over from one activity to another.

The training effect is even somewhat specific within running, with sprinting and distance running each requiring and producing different actions and reactions. How much speedwork helps a distance runner and how much endurance training helps a sprinter are still subjects of much controversy. But it is apparent that the bulk of one's training must fall within reasonable reach of racing distance, close to racing pace, or both, to be most effective.

4. **Principle of regularity:**

Almost any kind of running, in any amount, will yield some benefit if only it is taken regularly. Once a runner has the daily running habit, it's hard not to improve.

Physiologists say that runners need to train at least every other day—three or four days a week—to achieve and maintain basic fitness. Conditioning occurs quickly at first, with speed developing somewhat faster than endurance. But the reverse is also true. Conditioning vanishes quickly during layoffs, with speed diminishing somewhat more rapidly than endurance.

5. **Principle of progression:**

Obviously, progress is quickest and most apparent at the start of a racer's career, and it slows as one approaches maximum potential. The more the runner progresses, the harder it is to keep improving.

Progress, however, doesn't follow a smooth, upward course. There tends to be a "plateau" effect, with a series of sudden jumps separated by stagnant periods. The runner has to be prepared to work through these periods of no apparent improvement, waiting for the jumps. All else being equal, however, it is possible to hold the ground gained and move from strength to strength as condition and confidence increase over a period of many years.

6. **Principle of diminishing returns:**

The first mile is the most helpful one in terms of basic conditioning. Each succeeding mile yields less benefit. In other words, runners work more and more for less and less.

It doesn't take very much effort to reach ninety percent fitness—only a few miles a day. But you require progressively more training as you approach your ultimate potential until, at the highest levels, you're putting in a huge investment for very small additional gains.

7. **Principle of recovery:**

The interval-training system is more than simply mixing fast and slow running in a track workout. The principle of alternating effort with recovery applies to all training, regardless of the specific method used.

Forbes Carlile wrote: "Recuperation periods are essential, both during a single training session and throughout the year. Rest, with consequent physical and mental relaxation, must be carefully blended with doses of exercise. A rhythmical cycle of exercise and recuperation should be established."

Bill Bowerman, one of America's most successful coaches, pioneered what he called the "hard-easy" system. He staggered the intensity of workouts, scheduling a hard one only every two or three days. According to Bowerman, this allowed athletes to handle greater work loads with less strain, and stimulated faster improvement than a same-load-every-day plan.

All sound training programs leave room for rest and recovery. "There is a time for strenuous activity and a time for resting," Carlile cautions. "The rigidity of a too-definite program of training may easily drive the athlete to exhaustion."

8. **Principle of seasons:**

Sub-maximal training can be viewed as putting money in the bank; all-out racing as withdrawing those funds. No one can withdraw indefinitely. Eventually he or she must go back and restore the reserves. This explains the importance of racing sparingly during certain seasons and allowing race-free periods during the year.

Arthur Lydiard stated flatly, "You can't race well the year-round, because your condition will only take you so far. When you're racing hard, you can't train hard. If you compromise, you can hold your form for three or four months. But then you're going to have to go back and start to build up again."

If runners are lucky, Lydiard asserted, they may squeeze two peak periods of racing from a year, each lasting about three months and staggered with recovery breaks.

9. **Principle of pacing:**

Pace has two meanings. The first is obvious: the speed a runner travels during an individual run. The other is less apparent but just as important: the pace one maintains from week to week, month to month, year to year.

One principle rules both types of pacing: The harder and faster a person runs, the shorter he or she will be able to go. Fast pace lets you travel quickly; slow pace allows you to run longer. Set the training pace according to short-term (the distance of the run) and long-term (the projected length of the career) goals so as not to run down at the mid-point.

10. **Principle of individualizing:**

There can be no one plan suitable for everyone. Each program must be customized to accommodate the individual user's likes and needs, abilities and goals.

Forbes Carlile wisely said, "Always the most important consideration must be how the individual is responding to training, whether the athlete is carrying the physical load of training without strain or whether the body is slowly losing its capacity to adjust. Therefore training will always be an individual problem. No fixed training schedule should be followed rigidly. Blindly following any written schedule is unwise. For best results, training must be tailored to suit the individual."

CHAPTER TWO

In the Beginning

Fitness and Beyond

In the late 1960s, Dr. Kenneth Cooper presented us with the radical message that we should run more; we were suffering from inactivity. His aerobics books led millions of people onto the tracks and roads.

Looking back years later on the running boom which he helped inspire, Dr. Cooper observed that we runners might stay healthier and fitter if we ran less. In *The Aerobics Program for Total Health and Well-Being* (M. Evans and Company, 1982), he wrote, "Recent research has shown that unless a person is training for marathons or other competitive events, it's best to limit running to around twelve to fifteen miles per week. More than that will greatly increase the incidence of joint and bone injuries, and other ailments. On the other hand, less mileage will fail to achieve the desired improvement in the body."

Cooper and his staff at the Aerobics Center in Dallas were "overwhelmed" by the incidence of injuries in people running more than twenty-five miles a week. While a competitor may willingly take the risks associated with higher mileage, Cooper argued, the extra running first yields diminishing returns and eventually negative ones. For non-racers, he set minimums and maximums: no less than two miles, four times a week, and no more than three miles on five days.

Cooper's associate, John Duncan, remarked that people running five three-milers a week "have the same low risk of developing heart disease as someone running eighty miles per week." Cooper agreed: "If you run more than fifteen miles per week, you are running for something other than fitness."

Of course, most of you run for very good reasons other than fitness. Fitness, as Dr. George Sheehan has said, "is a stage you pass through on the way to becoming an athlete." You are probably past that stage.

Three miles may be the upper limit for absolute safety. But it may also be the lower limit for race training—as well as for attaching the runner firmly and permanently to the activity. Three miles or less, taken every other day as if it were a prescription item, will make you fit. Three miles and more, taken daily, will make you a complete runner.

If you want to shed a few pounds or prevent a heart attack in later life, observe the Cooper limit. But if you want to sample all that running has to offer, you need to run more. Three miles is about where running quits being simply an exercise and becomes a sport, quits being something you do to tone your body and becomes a vehicle for exploring the limits of your abilities.

As you begin your exploration, look realistically at what you are about to do and why. Be aware that racing has nothing to do with fitness as Kenneth Cooper defines it; the efforts involved are too great. When you train to race, you are no longer running to lose weight and keep your heart in shape (although those benefits still accrue). You're training primarily to immunize yourself against the stresses of the race so as not to be hurt too much by them.

The most obvious stress is distance, and your first task is getting used to staying on your feet for as long you plan to race. Most events last longer than thirty minutes, and many of them will require sixty minutes or more to finish. So you must form a daily habit of training at least a half hour and occasionally extend the length to an hour-plus. (If you aren't already at those time levels, Table 2.1 tells how to work toward them.) Only after you're running this far comfortably should you concern yourself with racing.

Graduating to Racing What follows is a case history of one race, the huge and zany Bay to Breakers in San Francisco. Many cities host similar events; every city should have one. There is no better way to take the long step from running to fitness to training and racing for sport than by joining this type of crowd.

One of the great exercises in the Bay Area, practiced by runners who call themselves "serious," is derogating the Bay to Breakers race. They say they can't be bothered by this event because it is too crowded, too chaotic, too crazy for them. They miss the point.

The crowds and the zaniness of this event (the word *race* somehow doesn't fit) help it serve its most important purpose: introducing masses of runners to the organized sport. More people come into racing via this twelve-kilometer route across San Francisco than any other single way—because more have run here than in any other single race. Of the nearly 100,000 people who run here each year, about half have never raced before. This introduction will prompt hundreds of them to move on to other, smaller and better events.

Table 2.1 Preliminary Steps

Two prerequisites should be satisfied before attempting any race: daily runs of at least a half hour and a long run of an hour or more. If you now are running less than these amounts, enter this program one step up from current level. For instance, if you're averaging twenty minutes (total time divided by seven, even if not running every day), begin in fifth week. Run at a pace that allows you to finish these runs comfortably. Record your actual runs by day and your averages by week.

First Week (Average: 13 Minutes)

Day	Suggested Run	Actual Run
1	15 minutes	_____
2	15 minutes	_____
3	15 minutes	_____
4	15 minutes	_____
5	15 minutes	_____
6	20 minutes	_____
7	Off	_____
	Daily Average:	_____

Second Week (Average: 15 Minutes)

Day	Suggested Run	Actual Run
1	15 minutes	_____
2	15 minutes	_____
3	15 minutes	_____
4	15 minutes	_____
5	15 minutes	_____
6	30 minutes	_____
7	Off	_____
	Daily Average:	_____

Third Week (Average: 18 Minutes)

Day	Suggested Run	Actual Run
1	20 minutes	_____
2	20 minutes	_____
3	20 minutes	_____
4	20 minutes	_____
5	20 minutes	_____
6	30 minutes	_____
7	Off	_____
	Daily Average:	_____

Fourth Week (Average: 20 Minutes)

Day	Suggested Run	Actual Run
1	20 minutes	_____
2	20 minutes	_____
3	20 minutes	_____
4	20 minutes	_____
5	20 minutes	_____
6	40 minutes	_____
7	Off	_____
	Daily Average:	_____

Table 2.1—Continued

Fifth Week (Average: 23 Minutes)

Day	Suggested Run	Actual Run
1	25 minutes	_____
2	25 minutes	_____
3	25 minutes	_____
4	25 minutes	_____
5	25 minutes	_____
6	40 minutes	_____
7	Off	_____
	Daily Average:	_____

Sixth Week (Average: 25 Minutes)

Day	Suggested Run	Actual Run
1	25 minutes	_____
2	25 minutes	_____
3	25 minutes	_____
4	25 minutes	_____
5	25 minutes	_____
6	50 minutes	_____
7	Off	_____
	Daily Average:	_____

Seventh Week (Average: 28 Minutes)

Day	Suggested Run	Actual Run
1	30 minutes	_____
2	30 minutes	_____
3	30 minutes	_____
4	30 minutes	_____
5	30 minutes	_____
6	50 minutes	_____
7	Off	_____
	Daily Average:	_____

Eighth Week (Average: 30 Minutes)

Day	Suggested Run	Actual Run
1	30 minutes	_____
2	30 minutes	_____
3	30 minutes	_____
4	30 minutes	_____
5	30 minutes	_____
6	60 minutes	_____
7	Off	_____
	Daily Average	_____

No event anywhere is so welcoming of newcomers. While other races limit their number of entries, this one seeks ever-larger totals. While others work to rid themselves of "outlaws" who run without numbers, one-third of the San Francisco field doesn't enter and no one seems to mind. First-timers feel wanted here, and they are.

These novices don't feel intimidated, partly because this isn't truly a race except for the one percent of runners upfront. The other ninety-nine percent are packed together too tightly to generate the speed which is the essence of true racing. It's said that people are still leaving the starting line when the first runners are finishing seven and one-half miles away. That's crowded!

New racers, who imagine that the whole world is watching them and waiting to laugh when they fall, take comfort in this crowding. It gives them a place to hide and an excuse for running slowly. The crowd gives them little choice.

Hardly anyone takes racing seriously at Bay to Breakers. This is a mobile party, a celebration of running. The best way to celebrate, as the folks in San Francisco like to say, is to "go with the flow."

No matter how big the crowd is, however, each runner is responsible for keeping his or her flow going. That requires preparation. Twelve kilometers is a tough starting distance under ideal conditions, and those in San Francisco are far from ideal.

Besides putting in the recommended amounts of training time (regular runs of at least a half hour and long ones of an hour or more), the runner must anticipate the Hayes Street Hill. This dominant landmark of Bay to Breakers climbs 200 feet between two and one-half and three miles, then descends steadily for the remainder of the course.

Anyone who arrives at this event with only flatland training is in for a shock. The climb up the hill will hurt immediately and intensely, but the long run downhill will do more damage to the legs. The advice is obvious: train on hills, practicing a steep half-mile climb and a gradual four-mile descent before race day.

By training this way, a first-timer learns something important about all races: they begin long before he or she steps to the starting line.

Exercising
of
Opposites

Fully Fit

Like most runners with roots in the 1950s and 60s, I once thought extra exercises were a waste of time. The calisthenics of football and army basic training were used more to discipline the mind than train the body, and we runners already had plenty of self-discipline. Hurdlers and sprinters might need these contortions, but distance runners' time was better spent running.

I thought I had put extra exercises behind me when I stopped playing football at sixteen, only to have them return during a few unpleasant months in the Army at twenty-two. For almost ten years after that, I didn't do a pushup, situp, or toetouch. Why bother?

Meanwhile, injuries began to nag me—little ones at first, the kind that don't stop you but nibble away at the joy of moving freely. I ignored these little hurts, and they grew into big ones—the kind that cause you to miss a day here and there, then several days, then whole weeks. Eventually I ran myself into foot surgery and still hadn't figured out why.

George Sheehan told me why. Dr. Sheehan, the medical columnist and philosopher-in-residence at *Runner's World,* casually tosses off lines that are the envy of anyone who writes. His wisdom emerges in the form of short, simple statements which are easy to read and hard to forget. The Sheehan "proverb" on the subject of runners' exercises concerns strength and flexibility. He said: "When you run, three things happen—and two of them are bad." The good one is that you become a faster and more enduring runner; you adapt to the kind of exercise you give yourself. But if you don't take any exercise except running, the bad things happen and, in extreme cases, may stop you from running as they progress.

The first of these is tightness of the backside, all the way from the heels to the lower back. If you're a long-time, long-distance runner and aren't taking corrective exercises, you probably can't bend from the waist with your knees straight and touch your fingertips to the ground.

The second bad effect is loss of muscle strength in the upper body and development of strength imbalances in the legs. Runners' arms, shoulders, chest, and abdominal muscles are pretty much just along for the ride; if they're neglected, they shrink. The front-of-leg muscles from the hip on down get worked, but not as hard as the ones in back; this accounts for the imbalances.

At best, then, runners aren't as fit as they'd like to believe if they lack flexibility and balanced strength. At worst, they're wide open to all kinds of injuries.

I suffered the injuries, as hundreds of other runners have, when I specialized too much in running. (This is particularly true for those of us who do little speed training; faster running returns some of the strength and flexibility that long, slow distance takes away.) I know now that exercises are a good investment, giving hours of smooth running for a few minutes of supplemental work. I now invest in it every day and now tell other runners to do the same.

Try this: First, bend over and touch the ground (even if only with the fingertips). Then do ten honest pushups and bent-leg situps. If you can't pass these minimum tests of flexibility and strength, or if leg injuries are eroding the fun of your running, you need to do more than run.

Balancing Acts Let's begin our discussion about supplementary exercises by saying what they are not. They are not directly related to performance, and they are not the best way to warm up. You improve your racing times by training better, not by lifting weights like a shotputter. You warm up best for running by running slowly for the first mile or two, not by stretching like a yogi.

So why bother with supplemental exercises at all? In a word, *balance*. Running's effects on the upper body are nil, so if you don't want to end up with the stick-like arms and the stomach muscles of a plucked chicken, you might want to adopt the habit of regular strength-building. Among the simplest and most effective exercises are old-fashioned pushups and situps.

Stretching is meant to counteract the tightening effects of running, and is therefore best practiced immediately after finishing. The muscles respond best to stretching after they have been warmed.

The five stretching and strengthening exercises in the accompanying figures have been chosen with both benefits and practicalities in mind. They can be performed within a five-minute period that can be inserted into your cool-down activities; they require no apparatus or props; and none of them asks you to lie down on the cold, wet, or rough ground.

Five minutes a day will keep you as strong, loose, and balanced as a runner needs to be. You're not training for ballet or body-building.

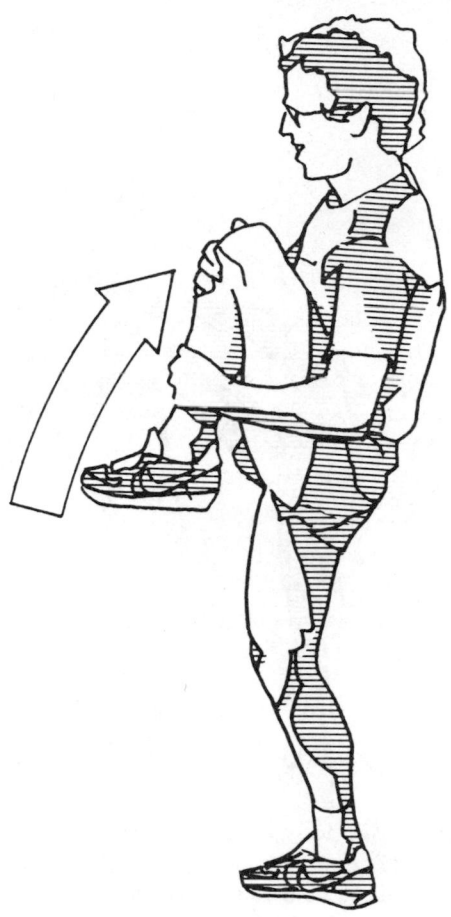

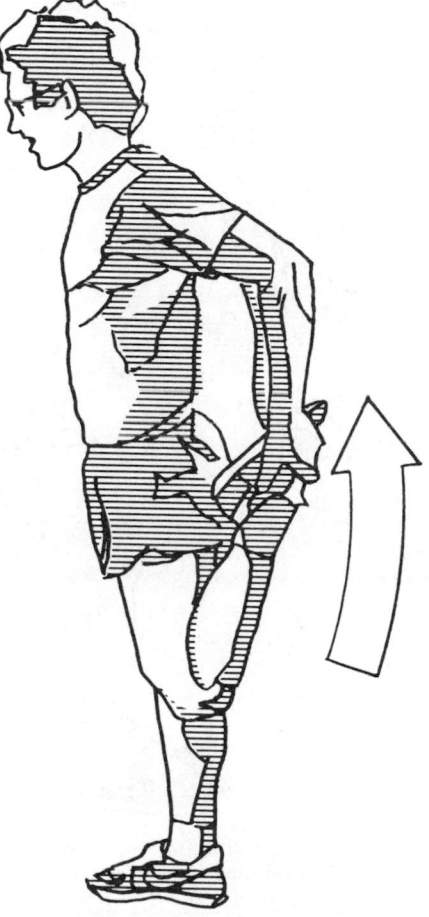

Part one: Cradle a lower leg and pull it toward chest.

Part two: Grasp a foot behind back, and pull toward buttocks. Repeat parts one and two with other leg.

Figure 3.1 The Leg Puller

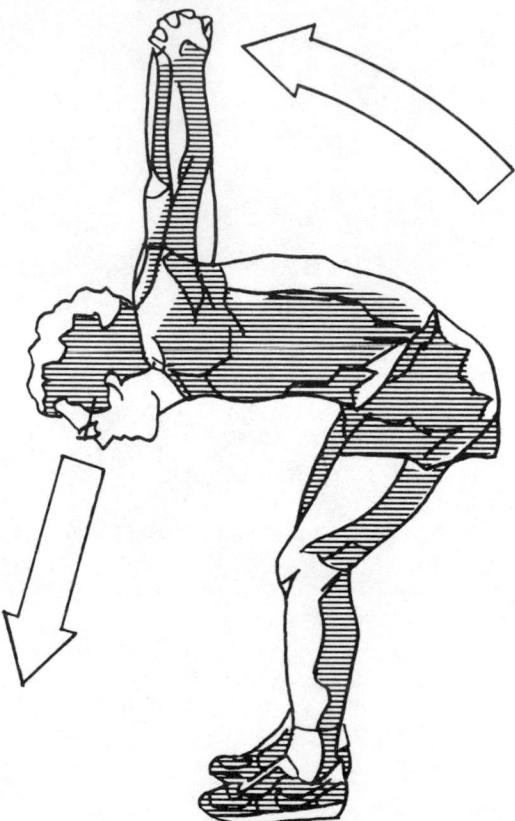

Part one: Clasp hands behind back, stand with feet together and knees slightly flexed. Bend forward while pulling arms upward. Stop at point of discomfort and hold.

Part two: Drop arms until palms touch ground in front of feet. The less flexible you are, the farther in front of the toes you will touch.

Figure 3.2 The Toe Touch

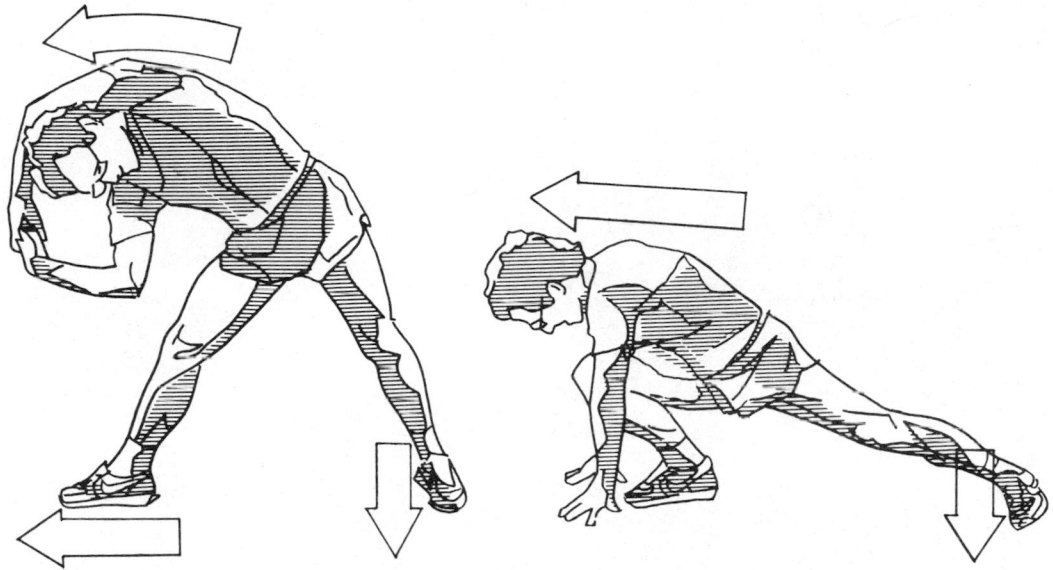

Part one: Stand with legs spread. Turn one foot outward, then bend in that direction.

Part two: Turn in the direction of bend, step forward, and reach as far ahead as possible. Repeat parts one and two on the other side.

Figure 3.3 The Triangle

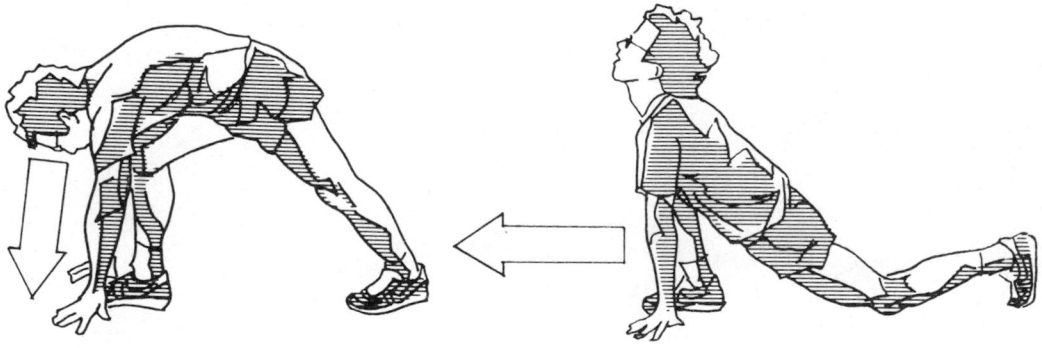

Part one: Crouch with one foot a few inches in front of other knee, hands on ground. Then straighten rear leg.

Part two: Step forward with front foot for an extended version of part one. Repeat both exercises with opposite foot forward.

Figure 3.4 The Sprinter

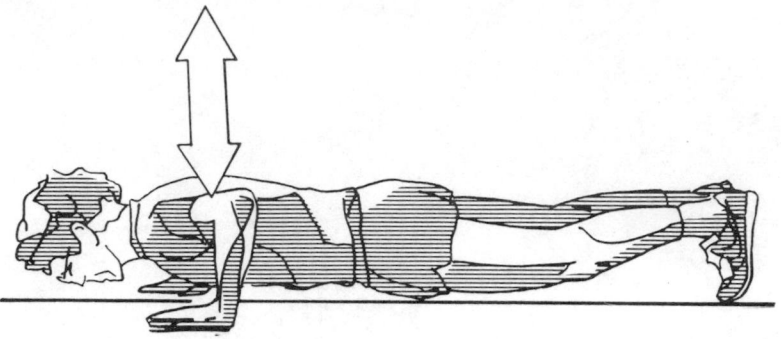

Standard pushup. From straight-armed starting position, touch nose, chest, and upper legs to floor, keeping back straight. Work up to 20 or more repetitions.

Figure 3.5 The Pushup

Training Table

Eat, Drink, and Be Wary

One hears contradictory dietary tales and ends up wondering what to believe. At one extreme, runners say they couldn't keep training and racing without their organic, unadulterated diets. At the other, Olympic marathoners report living on pizza and beer, and running on defizzed Coke. Diets of successful runners vary so widely—from vegetarian to vitamin J (for junk food)—that the normal conclusion you might draw is it doesn't really make any difference what you eat.

If diets are judged by the running results they give, "acceptable" eating habits obviously aren't limited to a few bland items. Runners can work well on a wide variety of fuels, and no one has yet determined a "best" diet for everyone, all the time. However, certain dietary adjustments do produce direct, measurable, and sometimes dramatic effects on running performance. Some involve adding items; others require taking things away.

The most important addition is liquids, particularly for long-distance runners. For events lasting more than an hour, drinks not only enhance performance but protect health itself. Marathon runners, for instance, need to drink immediately before and during races and long training runs. They can get by on plain water, but electrolyte mixtures put back more of what these runners lose.

Carbohydrate-loading—the popular practice of stoking up on bread, spaghetti, and similar foods prior to competition—adds extra fuel *before* the runner loses it. It is particularly beneficial in marathon running; researchers claim it can reduce a three-hour runner's time by as much as ten minutes. Carbo-loading is of little or no benefit in races lasting less than an hour, where performance is limited by factors other than fuel supply.

What runners *don't* eat is often more important than what they do consume. For example, the pre-race meal contributes little to the energy output of the event, and the potential for trouble is high when a runner puts food into a nervous stomach. Many runners prefer to go into their race hungry instead of risking the complications of eating too much, too late.

The big problem in nutrition is not *deficiency* but *overabundance*. Each pound above ideal weight (and "ideal" for runners is less than the figure shown on doctors' charts) is an extra burden to carry. It causes a drag on mechanical and oxygen-producing efficiency. The quickest way for most runners to improve is by losing a few pounds.

Weight is one of the most sensitive indicators of fitness, and all runners—whether overweight or not—should check theirs daily. Sudden gains, according to diet author Dr. Irwin Stillman, should be treated as if they were a serious illness. Sudden losses must be taken just as seriously. While a gradual reduction in weight is beneficial, a quick drop often signals trouble resulting from overwork, dehydration, or even true disease.

The runner's second-best training tool, after the digital wristwatch, is an accurate set of scales.

Last Suppers German doctor/coach/researcher Ernst van Aaken once remarked, "No one ever got fast by eating." Yet, as coach Arthur Lydiard pointed out, "The way runners eat before races, you'd think they were worried about dying of malnutrition after 50 meters."

The late Dr. Van Aaken thought runners shouldn't eat at all in the twelve to twenty-four hours before a race. They have all the stored fuel they need, he asserted, and putting more food into a tense system might cause indigestion, cramping, diarrhea, or other difficulties.

Van Aaken and Lydiard agreed that the best advice on eating immediately before competition is this: If in doubt, don't. This applies to the final hours before a race, when it is too late for the food to do much good but not too late for it to do harm.

The pre-race week is another matter. Evidence points to significant benefits from carbohydrate-loading during this period. This technique involves packing the body with high-energy fuel called *glycogen,* a product of foods rich in carbohydates.

The theory behind carbo-loading is that muscle glycogen supplies are limited. They are depleted in long races, causing us to slow down or stop. But these reserves can be built up by juggling carbohydrate intake, and we can go farther before a "collapse" occurs. The diet does not increase speed; it only delays slowing. It works best in races lasting longer than two hours, the point at which glycogen depletion would normally reach a critical stage.

The classic carbohydrate-loading routine involves three steps, summarized here:

1. A long "depletion" run seven days before the competition to drain the runner of glycogen.

2. The protein phase: three days of keeping the glycogen level low by eating high-protein, low-carbohydrate meals—meats, eggs, fish, etc.

3. The carbohydrate phase: three days of packing in the carbos for three days. (Don't interpret this as an invitation to overeat; maintain normal caloric levels.)

Paul Slovic, of the Oregon Research Institute, examined the results of "loading" in a marathon. He found that people on this diet typically improved by an average of eight minutes from their unloaded results.

The major complaint about the routine involves the high-protein phase. Runners say they feel exhausted and irritable then, and susceptible to illnesses and losses of confidence at the worst possible time. For them, a modified version of the carbo-loading routine gives some of the benefits while reducing the risks. They simply take the depletion run about four days before the race, then start loading immediately.

Whether or not you load with carbohydrates, you should examine the report of researchers from East Carolina University. This deals with what to eat—or more precisely, *not* eat—the day before a race. Dr. Ron Maughan, science columnist for *Running* magazine, reviewed the findings from the East Carolina study on rats:

> The authors of this report showed that treadmill-running endurance capacity can be increased if preceded by a 24-hour fast. The fast resulted in low values of blood glucose and also decreased the liver and muscle glycogen stores. In view of the well-recognized importance of these carbohydrate stores in determining the ability to perform prolonged exercise, the increase in endurance capacity seem somewhat paradoxical.
>
> However, in spite of the fact that resting glycogen levels were lower in the fasted animals, the glycogen content of skeletal muscle after the run to exhaustion was *higher* in the fasted than the fed rats. There was no difference in liver glycogen content at exhaustion between the fed and fasted groups.

A glycogen-sparing effect occurred, according to Maughan, and another energy-producing substance was recruited more heavily. He continued, "Clearly, the rate of glycogen utilization is much less in the fasted animals. However, they have a higher concentration of plasma free-fatty acids at rest and during exercise. These animals therefore conserve their limited glycogen stores by increasing the rate at which they oxidize fat"—a much more abundant fuel than glycogen.

Maughan cautioned that, while these results may not translate into human terms, they "may call for a re-examination of the use of the carbohydrate-loading diet by marathon runners"—particularly in the last day before racing.

I myself would stop short of recommending a full twenty-four-hour fast on the day before racing. However, I believe there is little to be gained from eating during those hours.

Drinks for the Road Bill Rodgers was on his way to winning the 1975 Boston Marathon, possibly headed for a world-best time. He was running at better than five minutes per mile, with a cool wind at his back.

Then Rodgers stopped, took a cup of water, stood in the middle of the road drinking it, and looked around to see if anyone was catching him. Two more times before the race ended Rodgers did the same thing. He explained afterward that he needed to drink and couldn't gulp the water while running.

This story says a lot about the value of drinking during long races. If a runner at world-record pace on a fifty-degree day needs to stop for water, then we all must need to.

Liquid replacement, or lack of it, has an effect on performance in distance races on any kind of day. When temperature and humidity are high, fluid loss can threaten health—even life itself.

Running doctors say that after you've sweated away about three percent (about five pints or five pounds for a person weighing 150 pounds) of body liquid, your temperature increases to the point where performance suffers. When sweat loss exceeds six percent of your weight, heat exhaustion or heat stroke are possible. The latter has killed more than a few runners.

What to drink? Water is the first priority, according to Dr. George Sheehan, *Runner's World* medical columnist. "The second priority is sodium chloride [salt], then potassium. These electrolytes, as they are called, are found in commercial 'ade' drinks."

Prepared drinks also contain sweeteners, on the theory that they provide quick energy. In fact, according to research by Dr. David Costill at Ball State University, heavily sugared drinks are slow to leave the stomach and may keep vital water and electrolytes from being absorbed as quickly as they are needed.

How often to drink? Dr. Costill recommends taking a pint ten minutes before the race, and a half-pint at ten- to fifteen-minute intervals during the run. If you wait to drink until you're thirsty and drink only as much as your thirst demands, he warns, you will become increasingly dry.

"Man generally relies on his thirst to control body-fluid balance," wrote Costill after conducting his initial tests on drinking while running. "Unfortunately, this mechanism is far from accurate. In laboratory tests that require about eight pounds of sweat loss, we found that thirst was temporarily satisfied by drinking as little as one pound of water."

Reduce that sweat debt. Drink up!

Dress
for
Success

Views on Shoes

An overrated rule is to provide the feet with the most protection that money can buy. The trend in shoemaking has been toward *more:* more padding, more support, more stability, more heel lift. However, you may be a runner who responds better to less. Two New Zealanders make a strong case for wearing the lightest shoes they can tolerate.

Jack Foster, fifty-two, has run hard for twenty years, completing a 2:11 marathon at age forty-one. Conventional wisdom insists that older bodies need more protection. Yet Foster prefers the least of all shoes.

"I was introduced to running over farmlands, where the underfoot conditions were soft and yielding, and one developed good strength and flexibility," he has said. "I ran in light tennis shoes, because there were no training flats in those days."

Jack believes those shoes forced him to learn proper running style: "We ran in those flimsy, light shoes and developed a 'feel' for the ground. We learned to land properly or got sore legs, since we couldn't rely on the shoes to absorb any shock. We got into a light-footed gait which moved us over hill and dale very effectively. I'm certain this [style] helped me stay injury free."

Even now, when shoe companies beg him to wear their latest high-tech training flats, Foster continues "to run daily in shoes most people consider too light even for racing."

It might be argued that he is one of the rare and lucky individuals born with perfect feet. Such is not the case with Anne Audain. If any runner has reason to give her feet maximum protection, it is Audain: an Olympic marathoner and former world record holder at 5000 meters. As a child, she could barely walk because of a deformity similar to clubfoot. Doctors corrected that when she reached her teens, and she started running as part of her therapy.

Those feet still aren't perfect, and Anne takes care of them in a most unusual way, as she once explained in a conversation with Bob Wischnia of *Runner's World*. Wischnia asked Audain how much her feet bothered her now.

"Sometimes they can be very painful and feel like they did before I had them operated on," she responded. "When it's cold, they have a tendency to throb a bit. However, they've never stopped me."

Does she wear special shoes?

"Heavens no! I race and train in the same pair of racing flats."

Racing shoes?!

"You have to understand that when I first started running, my doctors weren't too keen on the idea of it. One of them told me—and I think he may have been trying to discourage me—'If you're going to do this running, run in the nearest thing to bare feet.' Since that time, I've always raced and trained in the lightest shoes I can find."

While hesitating to recommend racing shoes for everyone, all the time, I do endorse several points made by the two New Zealanders. And I add a few thoughts of my own, as one who has always responded best to the least of all shoes.

- You're wise to wear the same type of shoes (if not the same pair) for all purposes, rather than switching models from training to racing. Raceday, the time of greatest stress, is not the time to risk a shoe change.
- You're built to run unshod, though modern surfaces no longer allow that luxury. Stay as close as possible to barefoot instead of removing yourself as far as possible from the earth.
- Light shoes enhance good running form. Heavy ones act as crutches which let the shoes instead of the feet and legs act as shock absorbers, thereby allowing the form to grow sloppy.
- If form improves in lighter shoes, but high mileage on hard surfaces still hurts you, maybe the fault lies in the running routine and not the shoes. Search the schedule for the trouble spot.
- The biggest drawback of racing shoes isn't the risk of injury but their cost. You usually pay more for less material and less durability.

Dressing Down Gone forever are the days of baggy, gray sweatsuits, cotton gym shorts and unmarked undershirts as standard running gear. Many contemporary races bear resemblance to sportswear fashion shows. Weatherproof jackets and pants (can't call them "sweats" any more), nylon mesh singlets (can't call them "jerseys"), and decorated T-shirts (can't call them "underwear") are all the rage. Runners who could once outfit themselves for racing for $25, counting the cost of shoes, might now spend ten times that much.

It's not necessary to spend that much. To be sure, some of the new items have made running more comfortable, but most of them are more fashionable than functional. You should concern yourself with function—with what effect your clothing has on performance.

Runners are most helped by what they *don't* wear. They more often overdress than underdress because they misread the temperature. They think the reading at the starting line will remain constant throughout the run or race. And it never does.

The human body works very effectively as a furnace, but rather poorly as an air conditioner. It creates heat better than it dissipates that warmth. As a result, the air temperature appears to rise by about twenty degrees during a run. A normally pleasant seventy-degree day soon feels like a steamy ninety. A near-freezing temperature rises to the pleasant fifties.

Dress with that "Twenty-Degree Rule" in mind. Feel a bit underdressed and chilly as you start, knowing that later you'll be cozy while runners around you are sweating in or stripping off their fashionable, expensive clothes.

Table 5.1 What to Wear When

Remember the "Twenty-Degree Rule": The temperture seems to rise by about that amount when you run. Dress with that warming trend in mind. Start with the basics of shoes, running shorts, and underwear; then, add layers according to the conditions.

Perceived Condition	Actual Temperature	Clothing to Wear
Hot	70s and up	Add only the skimpiest singlet (tank top) that modesty will allow; men may choose to go shirtless.
Warm	50s and 60s	Add a short-sleeved T-shirt to the basic uniform.
Cool	30s and 40s	Add long pants and a long-sleeved shirt or light jacket.
Cold	20s and down	Add a layer of protection for hands and ears, and perhaps another layer for legs and face in extreme cold.
Rain	Warm	Add a cap with a bill to keep vision clear; otherwise dress as on any warm day.
Rain	Cool	Add a cap plus a water-repelling jacket and pants; don't wear cotton "sweats" which soak up water.
Snow	Cold	Add extra socks to keep feet warm and dry; be sure the shoes provide adequate traction on slippery roads.

Reprinted from *Running for Fitness, for Sport, and for Life* (Wm. C. Brown Publishers, 1984)

CHAPTER SIX

How Far?

Time After Time

Ask me to name the single greatest advance in running during the recent Golden Age, and I'll talk about an attitude. I'll tell you that this sport boomed when dozens, then hundreds, then thousands of us decided running was too good to belong exclusively to young and fast males. We began to take running personally. The elite might travel longer and faster, but no one else could do our running for us—no one could break our PRs.

Ask me about the one great invention that supports this new attitude, and I'll point to my wrist. It holds a digital watch that has become as indispensable as shoes and shorts.

The watch is much more than a silicon chip wrapped in black plastic, and it's worth far more than its $21.95 price tag. This watch is a companion, a coach, even a conscience. It tells me what I have run, what I should run, and that I'm only as good as the run I take today.

Watchmaking technology is running wild. Manufacturers offer ingenious products that calculate distances and splits, count footsteps, and announce times. If you're easily bored while running, you can divert your attention with video games, radios, tape recorders, even tiny television sets built into watches.

But all I want to know is my time: the flickering black numbers between 0:00.00 and the day's stopping point. These readings are the most accurate measure of training effort, the most personal gauge of racing success, and the surest way to keep me living in the present.

My diary lists thirty- and forty-five- and sixty-minute runs, never four- or six- or eight-milers. Practicality led me to replace the mile with the minute standard. Running by time periods eases planning and record-keeping. For instance, I don't need to measure or follow courses, since an hour is an hour wherever it is run. And I never guess at distances, but simply look at the watch and note the elapsed time.

Running by the watch also encourages this ex-trackman to moderate his tendency to run too fast. My natural urge when running a set distance is to finish it as quickly as possible—*race* it, in other words. But because time can't be rushed, I settle into a comfortable pace during daily runs while training by the watch. That pace adjusts automatically to my day-to-day feelings, both good and bad.

Only in races do I dare allow distance and time to come together. There the whole purpose is to rush, and there the time is the truest measure of success. There the real victory ceremony occurs as the runner takes his or her first look at the result frozen on the face of the watch.

Times tell the truth. They say exactly what kind of runner I am, how I rank alongside runners everywhere, and—most importantly—how I compare with my old self. The current comparison shows almost a minute-per-mile slowdown from the PR years, and yet these are numbers I can accept.

Again, the digital stopwatch comes to the rescue. It gives visible proof that time doesn't stand still, and neither can I. No runner can hold onto precious moments for very long.

A man from Texas complained to me on the eve of his marathon, "I dread the next several weeks. I'll hurt for a few days, but that's not the half of it. The post-race blues will last much longer and will bother me much more than any stiffness ever could." He asked what he could do to ease the letdown he felt after every race. The longer the event, the bigger was the buildup and the harder the fall. Marathons were both the most exciting and most depressing events on his racing calendar.

"It's a matter of time," I said. "You look forward to the race for so long while you train that you're like a kid waiting for Christmas. Then it's all over in a few hours. Maybe those hours gave you what you wanted, maybe they didn't. Either way, they're gone just like that. The next morning, you wake up and see that you have little to show for your efforts except your pains and a line in your diary."

The runner nodded glumly, then asked, "But what can I do to ease myself through the blues?"

I tapped the black plastic watch on his wrist. "This is one of the greatest inventions in the history of running. It not only gives you the prize that counts most, an accurate record of your result, but it shows how fragile your prize is."

The man understood the first part of that answer but not the second, so I explained: "You put every number on that watch with your sweat. Wear the time proudly. Leave it on the face all day and night. Glance at it now and then, and smile as you celebrate your race.

"But pay special attention the next day when you zero that watch. This act tells you that the time has come to move on, to wipe away the old result and start putting new numbers on the dial."

Yesterday's races make sweet memories, but they don't take the place of today's and tomorrow's runs.

The 30-60 Formula Run far enough to feel you've accomplished something, but not so far that running seems like a second job. Most days, thirty minutes will satisfy the first requirement; sixty minutes is the dividing line between enough work and too much. Stop short of a half hour only when injured, ill, or taking a planned rest day. Exceed an hour only when you're preparing specifically for a race lasting that long, and go that far no more often than once a week.

This thirty-sixty formula is based on a rationale which we'll examine in a moment. But first, let's hear from the formula's detractors: the proponents of fitness who claim that even a half hour is too much to run daily, and the serious athletes who maintain that a steady diet of thirty- to sixty-minute runs is inadequate.

Graduates of the Kenneth Cooper School of Limited Mileage argue that even lower figures may be excessive, particularly if practiced without at least two rest days each week. Running this far every day is an invitation to injury, they warn.

Runners schooled on high-mileage training scoff at the one-hour limit. After I published the thirty-sixty formula in a magazine article, one athlete wrote: "The suggested training schedule is unrealistic. While I agree that recovery days are necessary, I don't believe that one hard day per week is sufficient training." He asserted that most "good to very good" runners exceed an hour at least every other day.

My recommendations fall between the extremes. Experience and observation tell me that most runners want, need, and can handle regular runs of a half hour or more, and that few of them can tolerate repeated runs of longer than an hour. To veteran runners, modestly paced thirty-minute runs become almost as easy as resting—and the more pleasant of the two alternatives. This running itself is a form of active recovery from hard work.

Extra-long and extra-fast training, and, of course, racing itself are the hard work. Precisely for that reason, a number of easy runs must separate the hard ones. We don't recover overnight, and we delay our healing by trying to put in too many miles at the wrong time.

Dr. Ron Maughan has addressed the question of what the recovery rates are from various amounts of running. Reviewing a Dutch study which used rats as subjects in assessing degrees of muscle damage, Dr. Maughan noted that "the exercise intensity was not severe and would correspond to a fairly moderate training session in [humans]." Results of the study indicated that thirty-minute runs on a treadmill caused no visible problem, while sixty-minute sessions produced significant signs of muscle damage. Healing began the third day after the trauma occurred and reversed itself completely a few days after that.

These experiments with laboratory rats lend scientific support to the arguments that hour-plus runs hurt and half hour runs don't, and that every day of hurting must be followed by many days of healing. It is important to note here that healing is not necessarily synonymous with resting. What it does mean is doing no further damage while recovery is taking place.

38

How Fast?

LSD Redefined

"Contrary to appearances," began my first book, which really was little more than a pamphlet, "I'm not attempting to establish myself as an apostle of LSD (long slow distance, in this case). I'm nothing more than a reporter, telling what happened to me and others who stumbled into this slow-motion running. This slim book contains a simple report of experiences from which you can draw your own conclusions, agree or disagree."

I neither invented nor named the LSD system: I merely wrote a booklet that describes it. Since the publication in 1969 of *LSD: The Humane Way to Train* (Tafnews Press, 1969) I have spent much time explaining to people who haven't read the original work what it does *not* say.

What LSD isn't:

- It isn't necessarily the best way to train. There are better ways to prepare for racing, but this is presented as an alternative for those who have tired of taking those harder, faster paths.
- It isn't mindlessly adding up mileage. Lengths of single runs and total distances should be the least you need, not the most you can tolerate.

- It isn't meant to be as slow as you can go. The ideal pace is neither too fast nor too slow, but fits into a comfort zone between the extremes.
- It isn't all long and slow. You learn to run faster by running fast, in small but regular doses of speedwork.
- It isn't surrender. You may even improve your racing performances, not so much by being better prepared as by staying healthier and hungrier.

LSD is running comfortably, both in terms of distance and pace. It is running at least a half-hour and no more than an hour, one to two minutes per mile slower than ten-kilometer race pace most of the time.

The system has served this long-time user well, but LSD is obsolete. Oh, I still believe enough in what I've done for the past twenty years to keep doing it. That's not the problem. The trouble lies with that name. Each of its three words urges extremism—something not intended for a system built on moderation.

The words *long, slow* and *distance* imply running as long as possible, as slowly as you can, adding up as much weekly distance as you're able. This can hurt as much as running too fast, as many runners have learned by taking LSD to extremes.

Runners who knew me in 1966, as my LSD phase was beginning, often asked, "Why are you running so much, and why are you going so slowly?" Runners who know me now say, "You run so little, and all of it is done at a fairly fast pace. Why did you change your LSD ideas?"

I haven't changed; the sport has. When I started doing what came to be known as LSD, runners still called anything beyond race length "overdistance." My thirty to sixty minutes a day seemed long. At a time when serious competitors still trained primarily on small, repeated parts of the racing distance and rarely ran them slower than race pace, even six minutes per mile seemed slow. My seven- to eight-minute pace appeared one step removed from walking.

I still run my thirty to sixty minutes daily; still run my miles at a comfortable seven to eight minutes apiece. I used to be so slow that no one would run with me, but now I pass nine runners for every one who passes me. Nine in ten of them run more than I do.

My running hasn't changed. I've stood still while the runners around me, their practices, and their perceptions, have passed through the distance/pace revolution.

Finding the Perfect Pace Take it from a racer who travels twenty times faster than the fastest runner does: Pacing is everything.

Johnny Rutherford drives the roads and tracks. In his kind of racing, pace doesn't just make the difference between good and bad performance. It determines, on one hand, if he goes home with a paycheck; on the other, if he goes home at all. The margin for pacing errors in cars traveling at 200 miles per hour is quite small.

Rutherford says that finding the right line between safety and speed is like holding a small bird in your hand. Hold it too loosely, and it flies away from you. Hold it too tightly, and you squeeze it to death.

He finds that delicate balance by driving at "red-line" pace. Hal Higdon, who writes about auto racing and the human variety, explains: "The red line is the mark on the tachometer of the racing automobile at which the engine, if constantly revved higher, will disintegrate. *Whoom!* Forty-thousand dollars worth of junk."

However, if the driver doesn't push that line, the race slips away from him. The same happens to a racing runner, of course. No one races well by pacing too easily. Yet everyone has a speed limit, beyond which lies disaster. Therefore, the first lesson in good racing is finding the line between fast enough and too fast, then holding it.

This is no secret. Racers who don't learn it quickly don't race well or for very long. And yet runners who tiptoe along the red line with the skill of Grand Prix drivers while racing may develop amnesia when it comes to carrying this lesson into training. The result? More races are lost in the spaces between events than in the competition itself. A runner lets good races fly away or squeezes them to death by ignoring the line between comfort and discomfort in the ninety percent of running time spent *not* racing.

Racing runners act like children spending a day at the beach. These youngsters may work for hours building elaborate castles of sand, then demolish their creations in a few seconds of gleeful kicking and stomping. They build to destroy.

Runners build for weeks or months in training, and then destroy much of that masterpiece they have created in a few minutes of racing—apparently taking great delight in this destruction. We, too, build so we can destroy.

In oversimplified terms, we use two gears: "running" and "racing." The first is rather easy to hold, and lets us run for *quantity*. The racing gear is hard to shift into and to tolerate once there; it allows us to achieve *quality,* but only temporarily.

To oversimplify again (ignoring the fact that some runners "race" their runs and others "run" their races), racing tears down. The problems runners who race have to solve are first, how to build more than they destroy, and second, how to rebuild adequately before destroying again.

We run for fitness. Running must be comparatively comfortable if it is to build and to last. We race for sport—not despite its destructiveness but *because* of it. Sport involves taking chances, seeing how far we can push before we break, gambling that we can bend without snapping.

Most of us want the best of two worlds. We want to run injury-free and enjoyably for the rest of our lives. We also want to race as well as possible. We can't have all of both at the same time, however, because the two goals conflict.

To run too easily is to risk racing slowly. To race too hard is to risk losing everything. Combining long-term, healthy running with immediate racing success requires careful juggling of quantity and quality—and a few compromises on both sides.

In the original LSD booklet, I offered the opinion that we build best by training at least a minute per mile slower than we race. I had no basis for that statement other than personal experience. On rare occasions when I checked everyday pace, it averaged that much more than long-distance racing rate.

Now I know that this guess was relatively accurate. Hal Higdon, surveying top road racers for *The Runner* magazine, found that the men were, as a group, 2:12 marathoners, while the women had run 2:35. These men averaged 6:07 mile pace in training; the women 6:48.

These times sound fast to those of us who have trouble *racing* at those speeds. But think of the times in relative terms: the men raced marathons near five-minute pace, and the women went below six.

There's that one-minute difference between training and racing pace for marathoners. The gap widens to about one and one-half minutes at ten kilometers and two full minutes for a single all-out mile. If these safety margins work for the best of us, they must also apply to the rest of us.

CHAPTER EIGHT

How Often?

Day by Day

If you run about ten kilometers a day, every day, a growing number of voices that ring with authority tell you that you're headed for trouble.

- *Item:* A now-infamous study from the University of Arizona implies that anyone who runs with an unusual degree of consistency and commitment displays unhealthy obsessive-compulsive tendencies.
- *Item:* Sports medicine author Dr. Gabe Mirkin comments that running is "the most dangerous exercise," and that "if you run every day, you're headed for disaster."
- *Item:* Evidence from the country's leading exercise physiology laboratory at Ball State University shows that people who continue training immediately after a race take about twice as long to recover as those who rest completely for several days.
- *Item:* Dr. Kenneth Cooper asserts that if you run more than three miles a day or more than five times a week, "you are running for something other than fitness."

Which is precisely the point. Most of you are past the stage of running purely for fitness. Three miles may be the upper limit for health maintenance, but it may also be the lower limit for race training and for attaching ourselves firmly to the sport.

The first thirty minutes of a run, says Dr. George Sheehan, is for your body; the extra time is for your mind. The first part is a warm-up for the good part. Three miles is the approximate point at which the exercise becomes a sport. And you take calculated risks in the name of sport.

Just so you won't think I'm advising taking foolhardy risks, let me say here that I accept without question Bill Bowerman's "hard-easy" concept. Alternating work with recovery is basic to any sensible running program. Each day of hard work must be followed by at least one and probably several easy days. Where I part company with the people who warn that we run too much, too often is over the definition of *easy*.

To George Sheehan, the word means "total rest." He once thought he had to train every day. To stay with that routine, he limited himself to about five miles a day. Any more than that, and he was tired and sore all the time.

Sheehan's racing performances leveled off, then began to slip. He is, above all, a racer; he wouldn't tolerate slowing down. So he tried taking a day off each week. He felt better, so he wondered, "Why not two days?" Feeling fresher yet, he dropped another training session to see what would happen—and then yet another.

What happened first on Sheehan's three-day-a-week program was that he could run more during each of his workouts. He both doubled the mileage and increased the pace on what became his Tuesday and Thursday ten-milers. The second effect was that his weekly races began to satisfy him again. At age sixty-five, Sheehan still regularly breaks forty minutes for ten kilometers. He has run as fast as 3:01 for the marathon on as little training as thirty miles a week.

This is hard-easy running at its extreme. The runs Sheehan does take last well over an hour each, are run at maximum pace, or both. Afterward, he forgets about running for the next forty-eight to seventy-two hours.

If you can stand waiting that long for your next run, you possess an unsual degree of patience. I'm not a patient man. I need my running more often than once every two or three days, so I compromise.

I can't race as fast or as far or as often as I once did without risking a breakdown, so I don't train for either miles or marathons anymore. And whenever I push to my present limits of speed or distance, I give myself at least an easy *week* to recover.

The compromise I make in the name of everyday running is that I *recover all the time* between race-like efforts. I rarely exceed ten kilometers of comfortably paced running. Ten-K a day keeps the doctor away.

One running course takes me past the local electric company's plant. Once a week, I check the sign at the gate reading "X Days Without an Injury." I keep this same kind of record myself. It has totaled as high as 1400 days.

This streak is not a bragging point. If maintaining it meant wading through injuries and illnesses, it would be foolish consistency. I am neither that tough nor that foolish.

What my streak means is that I've gone more than a year without *wanting or needing* a day off. I choose to think of this total not as a symptom of sickness, but as a sign of health: a sign that I've been doing lots of things right for a long time.

Our Hour Derek Clayton's stone wasn't aimed at me. He hadn't even heard my talk a few minutes before his, when I'd mentioned not missing a day's running in years. The former world marathon record-holder from Australia had been standing in the hallway, signing autographs and answering his fans' questions as I'd talked.

The same audience had heard both of us. These people heard me say I'd gone as long as four years without a day off. Then they heard Clayton say, "I know one bloke who won't even let himself have one day off. He runs right through everything—illness, injury, fatigue. That is bloody crazy. How can anyone have any fun in this game if he's so obsessed with it?"

Clayton did not intend personal criticism, but many of his listeners thought he did. As they stared in my direction, I wanted to crawl under my chair.

I had no chance to respond, but if I had replied my answer would have been one of agreement: "If I had to *force* myself to run through pain and exhaustion only for the sake of the streak, Derek would be right; I would be wrong. That would be an obsession, and those are never any fun.

"I enjoy my running. I like it enough to want to run day after day, and the way to continue day after day is to keep the distance and pace modest. I never let myself get so tired today that I can't run again tomorrow."

That means rarely running longer than an hour or within a minute per mile of current 10-K race pace. Few runners need to run or can tolerate running more than an hour or racing the clock regularly. The body and mind team up to shout, "Enough of this abuse!" Clayton had that problem.

One of the most ruggedly built men in high-level running, he still couldn't shoulder the training burden he heaped upon himself. Perhaps no one has ever trained more or faster than he did at his best. He went as high as 200 miles a week in training, most of those miles at or near five-minute pace.

And perhaps no top runner suffered more "down time." Clayton's medical history includes nine surgical operations. In spite of his record performances, he expressed some dissatisfaction with his career because it didn't net him an Olympic medal. His injuries occurred too often and at the wrong times.

When Clayton retired from marathoning after the 1972 Games, he made an incredible statement: "I can honestly say that I never enjoyed a minute of my running." He expressed relief at having put the suffering behind him.

It wasn't long, though, before Clayton began to miss his running. He didn't miss the racing, and he didn't miss the pain of his unrelenting hard training. The relief at being retired from those chores remained. But Derek missed something about the running itself.

He started again, this time averaging ten kilometers a day at a pace he could handle easily. For him, six-minute miles were easy compared to the five-minute pace at which he'd once raced and trained.

Clayton would start racing again, but never seriously, never again at his old distance and never with any special training. The man who once said he'd never enjoyed a minute of his running now calls his five- to six-milers at a comfortable pace a "highlight" of his day. That is exactly what the daily runs should be: a highlight, not a chore; a hobby, not a job; a time to be welcomed, not dreaded.

My own running became a dreaded chore twice. Early in my career, I ran too little and too fast. The ultimate price was an Achilles tendon damaged almost beyond repair and a damaged psyche that almost couldn't face another fast mile. Later, I ran too long and slowly, going two hours-plus every weekend and averaging more than an hour and a quarter each day. Its final result: heel surgery, which came as something of a relief when it took me off the high-mileage treadmill.

Only after settling into an hour-a-day routine did I feel I'd found my home. Only then did the running time become a highlight of my day. Once home, I didn't want to leave, even for a day.

I can't and don't fill those sixty minutes with running, but I can and do open up the full hour every day and run whatever I can within it. The best reason for taking that time has little to do with the physical results of the running. This is a quiet and creative hour when I call time out from the noise and confusion of the day, and spend an hour calming myself and collecting my thoughts. This would be a valuable and productive time even if one spent it sitting alone in a rocking chair in a quiet room.

CHAPTER NINE

Checks
and
Balances

Checkout Times

A reader chided me after he thought I'd advised in a magazine article to run an hour every day.

"You have excluded one crucial element," wrote James Menegazzi, a cardiac-rehabilitation specialist from Pennsylvania. "A day of rest. 'Rest' days have, oddly, come to take on the meaning of running for an hour at a comfortable pace. Whatever happened to the day off? One day off per week is not only refreshing; it makes good sense physiologically. If you have ever read Genesis, you know that even God took off one day a week."

I may never go so far as to *schedule* that day off for myself (although I suspect it might be a healthy practice). But I would surely neither preach nor practice running a full hour every day. Flexibility must be built into any program, or minor injuries will soon surface and evolve into major ones.

The best way to treat almost any ailment, from minimal ache to appreciable injury, is to do nothing. Nothing, that is, which produces any more pain. Never run with any pain or through any pain that interferes with the normal flow of the run.

"Run as you feel," the experts tell you. But how do you know how you feel? How can you be sure your head isn't lying to your body? One day, you might want to run for three hours when your physical limit is fifteen minutes. Another day, you may be able to go forever but don't feel like taking the first step.

I usually err on the long side, wanting to run more than I'm able. So I've adopted a set of checkout times that better match desires with abilities. My quarter-hour self-checks are outlined here.

- I start, unless it is painfully obvious that I'm going nowhere. Pre-run feelings, either good or bad, tell almost nothing about what to expect later on. The first fifteen minutes let me know realistically if I should bail out early.
- If no pains shout "Stop!" at that point, I go on to thirty minutes. Then I check out the main systems again, and call it a day if the run has become a struggle.
- With that test passed, I proceed to forty-five minutes. This is my usual stopping place, indicating a satisfactory run though not a great one.
- I continue to an hour only when all the gears are meshing perfectly. I know from many trials and errors that I can't or won't make a habit of going this far. That fact makes these rare days of overdistance extra-special.

When Running's a Pain A four-year streak, my longest period without a day off, ended on a crumbling bike path. I stepped the wrong way on a rough spot, and my left ankle went east while the rest of me kept going south. Diagnosis: Severe sprain. Treatment: A cast. Time off: Ten days.

I sulked for two days, which was the best therapy I could have practiced—both for early healing and to make myself thoroughly miserable. The complete rest made me so sick of inactivity that it built up my resolve to do something, *anything* active again.

Running was out of the question, but I have an active imagination. If I couldn't run, I could *pretend* I was running. I got up at my usual time, and went out for the usual time periods on my usual courses. The only unusual factor was the bicycle under me. I bicycled until I could walk without limping; then, I mixed walking and running until I was well enough healed that I didn't have to pretend to run any more. Anything felt better than nothing.

From negative experiences grow positive lessons. Those few weeks of pain yielded a plan for dealing with other bad breaks that inevitably disrupt running. Supporting it is a commitment to maintaining the thirty- to sixty-minutes-a-day exercise habit, even when a normal run cannot be done. The five stages of recovery, in sequential order, are presented here.

1. *Biking or swimming.* These activities are the alternatives for the most serious of injuries, those which don't even allow walking without limping. They take nearly all the pressure off most running wounds while still giving steady workouts.

2. *Walking.* Begin walking as soon as movement without a limp is possible, and continue as long as pain doesn't increase. These two limitations apply at all stages; the exercise should never aggravate the injury.

3. *Walking mixed with running.* Add brief periods of slow running to the walking—as little as one minute in five at first, then gradually decreasing the walks and adding to the runs.

4. *Running mixed with walking.* The balance tips in favor of the runs, but keep inserting intervals of walking—say, one minute in five—at this stage, when steady pressure can't yet be tolerated.

5. *Full-time running.* Approach it cautiously for a while, a little slower than normal, and with no tests or races until runs of thirty to sixty minutes have become a daily practice again.

By the Numbers After he won the 1968 Boston Marathon, Amby Burfoot coined a memorable phrase when he told about his persistent "fear of the precious minute," and how this compulsion to get on with another job sometimes kept him from doing all the running he could or should do. I admitted to him much later that I suffer from an opposite but equal complaint: a *fascination* with the precious minute that often drives me to run when I should be doing something else.

My whole running life is a numbers game, I told him. I give great meaning to what really are rather meaningless numbers. Most of them revolve around the watch.

- One minute or more faster than normal pace turns a "run" into a "race"; one minute or more slower than race pace defines a run as "LSD."
- Five minutes is the "time out" period—for breaks during long or fast interval work (race-like efforts which I call "tests"), for walking after a run, or for supplemental exercises.
- Ten minutes in every hundred—ten percent of the total—is a self-imposed limit on racing and race-like tests.
- Fifteen minutes—the warm-up period—determines how well or poorly the day's run will go. This also is my ideal length for intense speed sessions.
- Thirty minutes draws the line between fitness and sport; less than a half hour may make me fit, but more than a half hour makes me truly a runner.
- Forty-five minutes is my perfect run: long enough to be an honest effort but not so long that it does much damage.
- Sixty minutes is where running quits being recreation and starts resembling a second job. "Long" runs start here.

The flickering numbers on the face of a wristwatch run my running. Arbitrary figures tell me when to start and stop.

The only records I keep are the final daily readings on the Casio. Those numbers go into my diary as soon as I take my last step, and I don't erase the digital readout until I take the first step the next day.

I'm like a man lost in the snow who thinks he knows where a hidden path leads, but really can only see his footprints behind him. The trail of numbers gives me the illusion that I know where I'm going by looking at where I've been.

Keep it Simple Discus thrower John Powell's first rule of training: KISS. "Keep it simple, stupid." Any fool can complicate something simple, he says. But it takes wisdom to simplify something complicated.

I wouldn't call myself wise. But I am old in the ways that runners measure age: more than twenty-five years and 50,000 running miles old. One system that fails with age is memory, and complex formulas now confuse me.

So I keep my plans as simple. Nine days in ten (the non-race/non-test days) are distinguished only by what they do *not* contain.

- No hard/fast runs of race-like intensity.
- No short runs—"short" meaning less than thirty minutes.
- No long runs—counting anything above an hour as "long."
- No hard/easy pattern. I don't need to mix work with rest when none of it seems like work.
- No double sessions. Too much showering and changing of clothes.
- No peaking. If I'm running right and choosing the right races, I'm in shape to race reasonably well all the time.
- No tapering. If I'm not working too hard, I don't need to rest before races.
- No recovery runs. The pace of daily running adapts automatically for fatigue, and thirty to sixty minutes isn't long enough to hurt very much.
- No off-seasons. A runner who likes to run never wants to take a vacation from it.
- No days off. Almost all of the comments above apply here.

Your Training

Plan your overall running schedule by determining the following:

1. How Fast to Train
Indicate your most recent ten-kilometer race time or estimate your current potential at that distance. _____

 Calculate your average pace per mile, dividing the time by the distance (see Table 10.1). _____

That per-mile figure represents your current maximum pace for the approximate distance of your daily runs in this program.

 Indicate your current average pace per mile for a typical training run. _____

 Copy your ten-kilometer racing pace from above. _____

 Subtract your race pace from your training pace and list the result. _____

Table 10.1 *How Fast to Train*

Use your most recent ten-kilometer race result, or an estimate of current potential, as a starting point. Calculate its pace, then add one to two minutes per mile. That is your ideal training-pace range for daily runs lasting thirty to sixty minutes. The reverse is also true. You should be able to race the 10-K one to two minutes per mile *faster* than you train at that distance.

Your 10-K Race Time	Your Pace per Mile	Your Fastest Training Pace	Your Slowest Training Pace
30:00	4:50	5:50	6:50
31:00	5:00	6:00	7:00
32:00	5:10	6:10	7:10
33:00	5:19	6:19	7:19
34:00	5:29	6:29	7:29
35:00	5:39	6:39	7:39
36:00	5:49	6:49	7:49
37:00	5:58	6:58	7:58
38:00	6:08	7:08	8:08
39:00	6:17	7:17	8:17
40:00	6:27	7:27	8:27
41:00	6:37	7:37	8:37
42:00	6:46	7:46	8:46
43:00	6:56	7:56	8:56
44:00	7:06	8:06	9:06
45:00	7:16	8:16	9:16
46:00	7:25	8:25	9:25

Table 10.1 —Continued

Your 10-K Race Time	Your Pace per Mile	Your Fastest Training Pace	Your Slowest Training Pace
47:00	7:35	8:35	9:35
48:00	7:44	8:44	9:44
49:00	7:54	8:54	9:54
50:00	8:04	9:04	10:04
51:00	8:14	9:14	10:14
52:00	8:23	9:23	10:23
53:00	8:33	9:33	10:33
54:00	8:43	9:43	10:43
55:00	8:52	9:52	10:52
56:00	9:02	10:02	11:02
57:00	9:11	10:11	11:11
58:00	9:21	10:21	11:21
59:00	9:31	10:31	11:31

If the difference is less than one minute, you are training too fast. If it is more than two minutes, your training pace is too slow. The ideal training-pace range is one to two minutes per mile slower than the racing rate.

Calculate your ideal proper training-pace range by adding one to two minutes per mile to your current ten-kilometer race pace (see Table 10.1).

Fastest training pace (add one minute).　　　　　　＿＿＿＿＿＿＿

Slowest training pace (add two minutes).　　　　　　＿＿＿＿＿＿＿

2. How Far to Train

Indicate the current average length of your training runs (in miles). _____

Indicate the current average pace per mile of your training runs. _____

Calculate the typical amount of time (in minutes) spent training, multiplying the mileage by the pace (see Table 10.2). _____

If the amount is less than thirty minutes, you need to run more. If it is more than sixty minutes, your training should run less. The ideal range for daily runs (not including long or fast races or tests) is a half hour to an hour.

Indicate your fastest recommended training pace (see Table 10.1). _____

Indicate your slowest recommended training pace (see Table 10.1). _____

Calculate the shortest and longest distances (in miles) that you should run in the minimum half-hour time period, dividing thirty by your pace (see Table 10.2).

Shortest (running two minutes per mile slower than ten-kilometer race pace). _____

Longest (running one minute per mile slower than ten-kilometer race pace). _____

Calculate the shortest and longest distances (in miles) that you should run in the maximum one-hour time period, dividing sixty by your pace (see Table 10.2).

Shortest (running two minutes per mile slower than ten-kilometer race pace). _____

Longest (running one minute per mile slower than ten-kilometer race pace). _____

Table 10.2 How Far to Train

Distances covered within a fixed time period vary widely according to pace. For instance, a runner averaging six-minute pace will travel five miles in a half hour, while someone running ten-minute miles will cover only five kilometers in that time. To convert your times to distances, estimate your average pace per mile for the appropriate running period.

Your Pace per Mile	Distance Run in 30 Minutes	Distance Run in 60 Minutes
6:00	5.0 miles	10.0 miles
6:15	4.8 miles	9.6 miles
6:30	4.6 miles	9.2 miles
6:45	4.4 miles	8.9 miles
7:00	4.3 miles	8.6 miles
7:15	4.1 miles	8.3 miles
7:30	4.0 miles	8.0 miles
7:45	3.9 miles	7.7 miles
8:00	3.8 miles	7.5 miles
8:15	3.6 miles	7.3 miles
8:30	3.5 miles	7.1 miles
8:45	3.4 miles	6.9 miles
9:00	3.3 miles	6.7 miles
9:15	3.2 miles	6.5 miles
9:30	3.1 miles	6.3 miles
9:45	3.1 miles	6.2 miles

3. How Often to Train

Indicate the number of days on which you typically run each week.   _____

If the number is seven, make one of the days "optional" (to include a reduced amount of running, an optional activity, or rest). If the number is five or less, increase to six running days a week. Reserve one of those days for racing or testing. See Table 10.3 for a sample weekly program.

Table 10.3 How Often to Train

Make exercising a habit by planning to do something every day. That doesn't have to mean running seven days a week, and it certainly does not mean working hard each day. Mix training runs, races or tests, and optional days into the weekly recipe. *Training* is defined here as runs of thirty to sixty minutes (less than a half hour if injured or ill) at one to two minutes per mile slower that ten-kilometer racing pace. *Racing* is any all-out effort, and *testing* is running that mimics a race in either distance or pace. *Optional* days may include normal training runs, shortened runs, or alternative activities such as hiking, biking, swimming, and cross-country skiing. A typical weekly pattern might look like this:

Day	Running Plan
Monday	train 30 to 60 minutes
Tuesday	train 30 to 60 minutes
Wednesday	train 30 to 60 minutes
Thursday	train 30 to 60 minutes
Friday	train 30 to 60 minutes
Saturday	race or test
Sunday	optional

Write your own weekly plan based on training recommendations from Tables 10.1 and 10.2:

Day	Time	Length	Pace
1. _____	30-60 minutes	_____	_____
2. _____	30-60 minutes	_____	_____
3. _____	30-60 minutes	_____	_____
4. _____	30-60 minutes	_____	_____
5. _____	30-60 minutes	_____	_____
6. _____	race or test	_____	_____
7. _____	optional	_____	_____

TESTING

CHAPTER ELEVEN

The Rehearsals

Three-Part Harmony

Be warned: A writer using my name authored a number of books in the 1970s that still rest on some bookshelves. That Joe Henderson is something of a stranger to me now. He occasionally offered advice I would no longer take, let alone give. His books froze ideas in time like photographs in a scrapbook. The cold type on those pages doesn't move, but I do. My theories and practices have evolved. Not that the old ideas were wrong; the new ones are improvements on them.

That earlier Henderson wrote about LSD running, but I rarely put in more than forty miles a week. He praised steady runs, but I'm not above stopping and walking. He scheduled a long run on weekends and avoided speedwork except in races; I plan a fast run most weeks and rarely run longer than an hour. He advised alternating hard days with easy days. I follow a hard day with an easy *week* and sometimes two.

The earlier Henderson published a marathon training plan that built to sixty-plus weekly miles. I tell people to follow Jeff Galloway's program which calls for as little as half that much mileage, and will use it myself if the marathon bug ever bites me again. Jeff's schedule for that race (see Chapter 19) may be the best anywhere, and its framework can support any kind of program. Our talks at his Tahoe Trails running camps certainly have led me to replot my own course.

Galloway ran in the Olympics of 1972, but he doesn't spend much time these days talking with fellow Olympians. Jeff is that rare sort of elite runner who knows how to advise the little people about the sport. He maintains that most of us run too much without going far or fast enough. The routines are . . . well, too *routine*.

Perhaps you know someone unhealthily preoccupied with mileage totals. He or she must reach a sixty-mile-a-week quota. He or she avoids taking easy days or speed days, since they would eat into that total. His or her main purpose in running seems to be adding up mileage totals in a diary. The old Joe Henderson would have pleaded guilty on those counts. But I know now that more harm than good results from running too much on the days meant to be easy, and then ending up too tired or bored to do justice to the runs meant to be hard.

I wholeheartedly endorse three Galloway principles:

1. To race well, we must get used to the stresses of racing distance and pace.

2. Most of us can't tolerate and don't even require more than one hard day—race, long run, or speed session—each week.

3. We probably need and can handle no more than an hour's running on all the other days.

Better racing comes from combining harmoniously the three elements of running: races, long and fast rehearsals for racing which I call "tests," and recovery/rebuilding training between hard efforts. For the purposes of this book, the elements combine in roughly this manner:

- Training—the majority of mileage, taken at a comfortable pace, seldom lasting less than a half hour or more than an hour, intended for R&R (recovery and rebuilding).
- Testing—a transition step between training and racing, farther and faster than training but easier than racing; at least one day and preferably as much as a week of R&R afterward.
- Racing—much farther and faster (and therefore harder) than normal; followed by at least one week of R&R or one day per racing mile, whichever is longer.

We talked of training in Part One and will move into racing in Part Three. Here, the subject is *testing*.

Simple or Simplistic? In one of my magazine articles, I included my thoughts about three-part harmony, recommending no more than one race or test a week, mixed with at least six recovery-rebuilding runs lasting less than an hour. One reader took issue with this advice.

"I find your view of training overly simplistic," wrote W. R. Elkman from California. "Apparently you feel that your running improves with less than one hour a day of training. I suspect you are among a minority of runners—or perhaps you simply aren't competitive."

True, my improvement stopped a long time ago, and my instincts as a competitor have withered. I'm running to keep running now, and three-part harmony is as much a survival technique as a training program.

Yet at my competitive best, I ran that simple way—without really knowing what I was doing. The more "sophisticated," demanding methods which I graduated to and gave five years of fair testing yielded no better results and far more injuries.

Elkman continued, "Most of the good to very good runners that I know improve on high mileage (eighty to 120 per week) and genuinely follow a pattern of hard-easy days." They push themselves several days a week, he explained, not just the one that I recommend.

Perhaps that's true of the best athletes. But most of us aren't "good to very good." We don't have the ability, the ambition, the time, or the resilience to pile up impressive amounts of work.

I've never tried to advise elite runners. They obviously take care of themselves quite well without my help. I'm not concerned with how much work these people can tolerate, but how little the others can get by with while still going where they want to go as runners. I've seen a little hard work go a long way for a lot of of people. I've also seen too many runners work too hard, too often, and wind up not being able to run at all.

I've been one of each type more than once. Rather than recount the worst of times, let's look at the stories behind the best of times.

My two best years were 1961 and 1968. As a high school senior in '61, I knew next to nothing about modern training techniques. Instinct alone led me to run around a four-mile section of land most days, occasionally adding a few miles to a session. The pace was rarely outside my comfort zone of seven to eight minutes per mile. To this, I simply added a weekly race or time trial when track season arrived.

My early race results were dreadful after I ran nothing fast all winter. I was lapped in my first indoor mile. But by season's end less than two months later, I'd improved my mile time by twenty-six seconds, won state championships in the mile and half-mile, and set a three-mile PR which would never be broken.

Five years of more complex and much harder training yielded only marginal improvement in the mile, my main event—and a growing amount of down-time for recovery from injuries. Only after I returned to my original, simple way of training did my health improve and times go down again. My running in 1968 involved little more than modestly paced thirty- to sixty-minute runs mixed with regular racing and simulated races at a wide variety of distances. Yet I came very close to the one-, two- and three-mile records I'd set as a fanatical kid, and ran all-time bests at almost every distance between six and twenty miles. Throughout that entire year, I lost not one day to injury or illness.

Much later, while reviewing the ups and downs of a long racing career with perfect hindsight, I discerned a clear pattern. If race-like effort (both true races and what came to be known as tests) totaled less than five percent of a month's running, I didn't race well; I felt sluggish. If the percentage went much beyond ten, I was too tired to race well and was courting injury. Racing five to ten percent of the time gave the best results and preserved the greatest level of health. Ten is my magic number: ten percent of total running taken as racing or testing, one minute or mile in every ten, a monthly average of one hard day in ten.

I list ten only as a starting point for your analysis. Your magic number eventually may be different, but that doesn't matter. The thing to remember here is the pattern of three-part harmony. Mixing training, testing, and racing in the right proportions may bring back harmony to a routine that has gone flat.

Hard and Fast Rules (Or How to Race and Test Often and Fairly Well without Really Suffering)

1. Treat racing and testing as prescription items. Taken in carefully measured doses and intervals, they give pleasant and predictable results. Underdose, and you get little benefit. Overdose, and you risk losing everything.

2. Count efforts as race-like whenever you time yourself for a measured distance and spend an unusual amount of effort on it. Races don't have to be official to take a race-like toll.

3. Don't mix training and racing, but do let training set your racing limits. Do no special speed or distance work on non-racing/non-testing days. Rarely race or test at more than two minutes per mile below the average pace or more than twice the average daily distance.

4. Don't race or test if you are ill, injured, or just don't feel in the mood for it. Leave the heroics to the heroes who race as if there were no tomorrow.

5. Make no firm promises as to pace or final time. Let them come as surprises. Goals preclude the element of surprise because you either reach them as expected, or fail and get frustrated.

6. Time the warmup according to the racing or testing distance. The shorter the race, the longer the preliminary run, and vice versa. In any case, total at least the daily minimum of thirty minutes.

7. Start cautiously and then accelerate, regardless of distance, attempting to run the two halves in equal time or the second slightly faster than the first. Give away a little time in the early going, knowing you'll probably get it back with interest later.

8. Leave the deepest reserves untouched. Rarely, if ever, go all the way to the bottom of the well. Stop before reaching the "survival-shuffle" stage.

9. Recover quickly and slowly. You should feel good enough to run almost normally the next day, but allow a week or more before racing or testing again.

10. Treat the race or the test as a bonus, not as the sole reason for running. Don't let the racing and testing taint the other ninety percent of runs.

Test and Rest

Pretending to Race

Test is a blanket term covering long runs, speedwork, and time trials. These are dress rehearsals for racing. By necessity, the tests are hard work. They lead up to the even harder work of racing.

Long tests mimic the distance of the race but at a slower pace. Fast tests prepare you for the race's full speed but cover only part of its distance. You combine full distance at full speed only in the race itself.

The long test at least matches the time (not necessarily distance) of the longest race you plan to run, but is done a minute or so per mile slower than racing pace. For instance, as a 1:30 half-marathoner (about 7:00 pace) you would run one and one-half hours or more at eight minutes per mile or slower.

The fast test at least matches the pace of the shortest race you intend to enter, but lasts no more than half the racing distance. Say your lower limit is 10-K, which you race in about forty minutes (6:30 pace). You'd test at a 6:30 or slightly faster rate, for 5-K or less.

The idea, then, is to bring together the two factors—full distance at full speed—in the race, where it counts.

These tests are race-specific. They get a runner ready for a single race or set of distances. In later chapters, I put you on one-month cycles: usually a long test, a fast test, a race, then an easy weekend. If the race requires a special build-up of speed or distance—such as a mile or a marathon—the cycle may be longer.

If, like me, you simply enjoy the feeling of going longer or faster, try more general forms of testing which key off from your typical daily runs.

- *Double-time:* Up to twice your daily average time or distance, at normal training pace. If you usually run up to an hour's worth of eight-minute miles, test for as long as two hours at 8:00 pace.
- *Half-fast:* No more than half your daily average, at one to two minutes faster than normal training pace. If you usually run at least a half hour at 8:00 pace, drop to fifteen minutes at six to seven minutes per mile.

In both long and fast tests, consider exercising the interval option. Interval training allows you to run longer and faster than you otherwise could or would. Intervals can be particularly valuable when you're breaking into the higher ranges of distance and speed—say, more than double your normal training time or more than two minutes per mile faster than typical training pace.

- *Extra-long tests:* A five-minute break every half hour can as much as double your longest non-stop distance with little increase in effort. That is the Tom Osler Rule, and it works. Example: The intended testing time is two hours. Run twenty-five minutes, call a five-minute time out (most commonly for walking but sometimes for stopping and stretching). Repeat that cycle three more times to fill the allotted period.
- *Extra-fast tests:* Mixing fast portions with recovery walks, in classic interval fashion, allows you to run faster with no great increase in stress. Example: The test totals a mile on the track. Run a fast lap, then click off your watch while walking a lap. Repeat this process as you take a cumulative time for the mile, not counting recovery periods into the time or distance total.

Passing the Tests Like most of us who write about running, Marlene Cimons of the *Los Angeles Times* would trade a dozen by-lines for one personal-record time. She once called me, not to discuss an article she was writing for the magazine that employed us both, but to ask the question: "How do I improve my speed?"

Cimons had run her first marathon. Now she complained of feeling she could run forever, but that her times in the 10-K had stalled.

"How do I get off this plateau?" she pleaded.

I told her to go to the track for an introductory course in speed: "Run at or near your fastest mile pace. But to keep from tearing yourself apart, divide the mile into its four laps and walk a lap between. Just time the fast parts, and keep a record of what those mile times are." She called with weekly reports on her speed sessions—first telling me how tired and stiff they left her, later saying how she could run better times with apparently less effort.

After her next race, Marlene could hardly wait to let me know that she'd run almost "three minutes!" under her old 10-K best. She'd done it simply by testing herself with one mile a week for six weeks.

People who've done the least fast running improve the most when they add a small amount of it. The same effect applies to long-distance testing.

After running her fastest 10-K, Marlene Cimons set out to improve her stagnant marathon time. She turned to another experienced runner for advice. Jeff Galloway, a former U.S. Olympian, told her to make just one change in her program. Once every week or two, she should take a long run which gradually increased in distance to the full projected time (about three and one-half hours) of her marathon.

When Galloway sends marathoners into dramatic increases in their distances (often tripling their longest runs within a few months), he advises them to ease the stress the same way I'd told Cimons to make speedwork more tolerable. That is by employing one of the most discredited and least used secret weapons: walking breaks. In pre-marathon tests, the walks commonly amount to about five minutes every half hour.

Nothing changed for Cimons except the length of her long run and the way she took it. She ran quite moderately on weekdays, little more than would be recommended for fitness runners. Yet she improved her marathon time by nearly ten minutes.

She raced much faster than ever before at both the shortest and longest distances because she satisfied the two basic testing requirements: frequent runs at or below race pace, but at a shorter distance, to develop speed; and regular runs of race length, but at a slower pace, to develop staying power. Marlene Cimons' case also illustrates dramatically that the quickest way to race faster and farther may be to start walking.

Walk Talk *Walk*. It's a simple word for a noble act, but most runners don't think the word belongs in their vocabulary or the act in their program. They're wrong.

Most of us equate walking with quitting, but I think of it as a small miracle. Selective walks permit us to go longer and faster than we otherwise might—and with less effort and pain. This is the purpose of tests: to mimic the speeds or distances of races without absorbing their stress blows full force.

Tom Osler, a largely unsung genius in matters of running technique, wrote in his *Serious Runner's Handbook* (Anderson World Books, 1978) that any runner can immediately double his or her longest previous distance without doubling the effort. The trick: splitting up the run with five-minute walking breaks.

Dick Buerkle, two-time Olympian at 5000 meters and former world record-holder for the indoor mile, says the quickest way to build speed safely is to run a fast mile. This is the special type of mile that Marlene Cimons used: four individual laps on the track, each separated by a lap of walking (which again takes about five minutes).

After I repeated Osler's advice on walking in a magazine article on marathon training which recommended a twenty-five-minute run/five-minute walk formula, reader F. Gregg Bemis from New Mexico wrote with three questions. After expressing the usual runner's reluctance to walk, he asked three questions: Is there anything particularly sacred about the mix of twenty-five/five during the longest training runs? At what point, if ever, does one wean oneself from the walks? And, if one's last long run before a marathon included regular walks, does this mean he or she should walk during the marathon?

I prefaced my response to this reader's question by first advising him to think of walking as long-distance interval work. The intent of intervals is to cut up a big chunk of work into smaller and more manageable bites. In this case, they allow you to cover more total mileage at a faster pace than you could with straight running. I then went on to answer his specific questions.

The twenty-five/five formula isn't chiseled in stone. Experience has taught me that a five-minute break is long enough to provide some recovery, not so long that it has a stiffening effect. Your trials and errors may tell you otherwise. The frequency of these breaks depends upon how often you think you need them.

Wean yourself away from the walks only when you can run comfortably the full time of your next race and can recover from the test effort quickly. Most limited-mileage marathoners never reach this stage.

During long-distance testing, you rehearse the distance and pace of the race while still not shouldering their full workload. Save that experience for race day, when you start with every intention of running every step.

The plan for making a speed breakthrough without breaking down is similar. Dick Buerkle discussed it on his "Running People" show for CNN Radio. Run 440s, he advised runners who don't normally indulge in speedwork. Run just four of them and walk—don't run—a lap between.

"Some people think they should do more than four repeats," Buerkle remarked. "I like doing only four, because you can run close to top speed without worrying about saving yourself for, say, the ninth or tenth sprint. We're talking about quality here, not quantity." He recommended walking instead of jogging between intervals, because "if you have a walk to look forward to, your mind is free to concentrate on blasting the running part."

Whether the test is very long or very fast, the walk is the pause that refreshes.

CHAPTER THIRTEEN

Running Farther

Climbing "The Wall"

It isn't necessary for you to be a marathoner to learn from the marathoners. Their lessons here deal with how far you need to run and how best to run that far.

Several years ago, I wrote a schedule for first-time marathoners. *Runner's World* published it in 1977, and the program enjoyed several reincarnations in magazines and books. That plan held the conventional wisdom of marathon training in the late 1970s. It emphasized rather high mileage, while claiming it to be "the least a runner can do while avoiding The Wall." It gave more attention to raising the average length of runs than to extending the long one. It contained one hard run a week and two more of medium difficulty.

The long run peaked at two and one-half hours (less than twenty miles for most runners), the medium two at one and one-half hours each. The important feature of the program was thought to be that daily average, which reached well beyond an hour.

My marathon plan drew heavily upon the teachings of Ken Young. A man of limited talent, Young developed himself into a runner of American-record caliber. As befits one who now directs the National Running Data Center, he analyzed meticulously his own and other runners' statistics. One result was the "collapse-point theory."

"Collapse point," wrote Young in the mid-1970s, "is the maximum distance a runner can expect to go before the urge to slow down overwhelms him. More commonly, the collapse point is called 'The Wall' (which one runs into) or 'The Bear' (which jumps on one's back). It is characterized by a sudden decrease in performance, often occurring within a single mile. Pace may drop off by two to three minutes per mile or more." In other words, runners must train themselves to complete a distance without "collapsing" before they can hope to race it. As racing distances grow, just getting through them is increasingly difficult.

Much of the training for long-distance racing, according to Young, simply involved building the ability to go the distance. But without a strong foundation of endurance, speed-work would be irrelevant. Speed couldn't be used if you were unable to lift your feet in the last miles of the race.

The collapse-point theory held that endurance limits were drawn by the mileage habitually run in training. Required distances depended upon the length of the race. You could finish a 10-K on as little as two or three miles a day. Marathoners, on the other hand, required eight or ten a day for an extended period to get ready for their 26.2-mile race.

Young worked out a formula which predicted when a runner would reach his or her collapse point. In simple terms, the formula stated that a runner would stop or slow down dramatically at a point about three times his or her average daily distance for the past month or two. If an individual were averaging thirty-five miles a week during that time (five miles a day), his or her projected collapse point would be five times three, or fifteen miles. That runner could count on getting through a half-marathon rather comfortably. But to try a marathon would be an invitation to the trouble that lay at The Wall and beyond.

Young advised training at least a third of the racing distance daily, perhaps even little longer than the minimum, to give oneself a safety margin. A marathoner, for instance, might average nine miles a day. Tripling that amount would move the collapse point out beyond marathon distance, to twenty-seven miles. The farther above minimum mileage one went, the less he or she needed to worry about breaking down and the more he or she could dream about breaking personal records. That was the theory. How did it work in practice?

Quite well, according to Paul Slovic of the Oregon Research Institute, who studied runners at the Trail's End Marathon. By questionnaire, he asked their training mileages for two months before the race and compared those figures to their marathon times.

Those who ran the most generally raced the fastest. Slovic divided the subjects into four groups: (1) the sub-three-hour runners who averaged nine miles a day; (2) the 3:01 to 3:30 runners who ran six miles a day; (3) the 3:31 to 4:00 people who ran five miles daily; and (4) those who ran slower than four hours and who typically ran only four miles.

Using the Ken Young formula, only the first group was adequately trained for a marathon. The other groups would have had predicted collapse points of eighteen, fifteen and twelve miles, respectively. If Young's theory were valid, these undertrained runners should have slowed down dramatically after meeting their "Walls."

Slovic's data indicated that this was the case. Even Group One's pace dropped, by an average of fourteen percent, from twenty miles to the finish. This compared with a twenty-two-percent slowdown for Group Two, thirty-seven percent for Group Three and fifty-eight percent for Group Four.

To interpret these statistics another way, the sub-three-hour runners lost only about five and one-half minutes (relative to their twenty-mile pace) in that last stretch, while the four-hour-plus marathoners used up nearly thirty extra minutes on those last 6.2 miles. Their pace by then was a thirteen- to fourteen-minutes-per-mile shuffle.

Several years ago, I believed that the way for runners to collapse-proof themselves was to work from the bottom: push up the length of the day's runs until they averaged one-third of the racing distance. That principle formed the basis of my old marathon schedule.

The Galloway Way The old program wasn't a bad one. It certainly was better than having no plan at all, which was how most marathoners had previously groped their way toward their first race. Hundreds of people wrote to say they'd used the schedule, and ninety-eight percent of those who completed the program also completed their marathons.

This schedule worked most of the time: I have a file drawer full of unsolicited letters to prove it. But I have retired that plan in favor of a new, improved model that is both simpler and safer. It closely resembles Jeff Galloway's, since our lessons come from the same source: other marathoners putting themselves on the line for the first time.

Galloway and I advise runners from the safety of a speaker's platform or a printed page. Those men and women themselves must breathe life into the schedules, and they suffer when the numbers we give them are too high or too low. When those runners speak, I listen. In general, they had two complaints about my old program. First, it sometimes asked them to work too hard. The medium-long mid-week runs required for pushing the weekly mileage total above sixty seemed particularly draining and difficult to face. Second, it didn't ask them to work hard enough at other times. The long, weekend runs, which peaked at less than twenty miles, didn't seem to prepare these runners either physically or mentally for the surprises to come in the most difficult part of the race.

Some of them told me they were stopped short of the marathon starting line when the heavy weekly mileage total broke them down. Others said they hit "The Wall" in the marathon because they hadn't approached this distance in training.

Once the problems were noted, the solutions were obvious. Add distance to the long day; subtract it from the other days.

How far should the longest run be? Galloway's answer is simple: as long as the race. While Galloway accepts the collapse-point theory in principle, he uses a different method for establishing it. He says runners are likely to find their racing "Wall" at the point where their *longest testing run* ends. One who has trained no longer than two hours will have a very hard time racing beyond two hours, while one who has gone three hours will know the third hour of a marathon as familiar territory.

How often to run long? Galloway advises doing it once a week at most, and only every other week when distance totals are climbing rapidly toward marathon level. Take plenty of time to recover in between with no runs of more than an hour and most of them far less. Don't bother counting total mileage, since that raises the temptation to run too much on the days meant to be nice and easy, resulting in not being able to run enough on the days intended to be good and long. The run that counts is the long test.

Ken Young's collapse-point formula still has merit. It lives on here in a modified form, as a testing tool. The old Young rule now tells how long to test and how to test long. Results of those tests then determine racing limitations.

Normally, the long-distance testing should not exceed three times the daily training amount (calculated from at least the past month). Better yet, think of double the average as the safe limit. A forty-minute-a-day trainer, for instance, might go as far as two hours, but would run fewer risks by staying in the 1:20 range.

If you must go farther than this formula allows, consult Table 20.1. It explains how to cheat the collapse rule.

CHAPTER FOURTEEN

Running Faster

More from Less

Three letters arrived, independently and unsolicited, the same week that Brooks Johnson sounded off against LSD training in *The Runner* magazine. The coach of the 1984 U.S. Olympic women's team had written: "Long slow distance is fine—for those who want to run long and *slow*. But American competitive distance running has been held back for more than a decade by dependence on long slow distance at the expense of speed. Speed must be the centerpiece of any intelligent training program for the competitive runner—at any distance."

As if in response to an article they hadn't yet read, Elizabeth Stronge, Ted Fulton, and Richard Stiller told how they had combined adequate but unspectacular amounts of gentle running with small doses of speed to produce the best results of their long careers.

Elizabeth Stronge wrote from Alabama: "Previously in preparing for the 10-K season, I ran once a week with a male friend, and we went at a fairly fast clip. I found myself a little sore from those days and also a little hoarse from telling him to slow down.

"This season, I decided the speed necessary for a decent (whatever that means) 10-K was not worth those uncomfortable speedy runs. So I took the opposite road and slowed down my training runs to pure 'pleasure' pace. I also added some swimming. I found myself suddenly stronger.

"To my surprise, I ran a 35:22 10-K and felt wonderful. (I usually run a high thirty-six at my peak.) My legs were loose and eager, and somehow I gathered my speed from the strength I had built on the long, slow runs. I accelerated through the fourth, fifth and sixth miles rather than gradually running out of gas.

"I tell myself my training runs are just for building back up; I get enough tearing down in the races. Whenever I run with anybody, I just say, 'I'm going easy today,' as if I had run twenty quarters on the track the day before. Sometimes they take off without me, rarely do they believe me when I tell them how little speedwork I do. Who cares?"

Ted Fulton wrote from Florida: "I had been training and racing almost constantly since 1978. I had run twenty marathons and over 200 races of lesser distance. I went to Jeff Galloway's running camp seeking a method of improving from a level of performance at which I had been stagnant for the past year or two.

"While I respected Jeff's diagnosis of my overtraining and streak (twenty-six months without missing a day) having me in a burned-out state, I felt compelled to keep pushing until after the New York Marathon.

"Unfortunately—perhaps I should say *fortunately*—my Achilles tendon would not accept the wait until its promised post-New York rest. Most of that fall and early winter were spent seeking quick and miraculous cures, and alternating rests periods and easy running.

"When I was again able to run regularly, I decided to apply what I'd learned from Galloway and adopt a new program which would no longer have weekly mileage as its goal. I abandoned my normal eighty-five- to ninety-five-mile-weeks, two-workouts-per-day, two-long-runs-per-week routine in favor of a twenty-four- to twenty-five-mile run every other week, with races on alternate weekends. To my amazement, I approached both the long runs and the races with a refreshed and enthused feeling.

"Leading up to the Boston Marathon, I had set PRs for 8-K, 15-K, 10-K and 5-K. But I still had reservations about the fact that I'd averaged only fifty-five miles per week.

"Those doubts vanished early in the race. I ran three minutes faster than ever before, the last mile was the fastest, and I had never felt so good during or after a marathon."

Richard Stiller wrote from California: "I was and still am a believer in long, slow distance. I have never done well on extended interval training but have consistently produced good times (for me) on ninety to ninety-five percent LSD, with races for speedwork every second or third weekend.

"In the past few years, I have adopted a slight variation in my training that usually leads to a successful string of races. Three or four weeks before my first race, after running almost pure LSD (fifty to sixty miles a week at 7:00 to 7:30 pace), I insert a sub-maximal interval workout into my weekly schedule. It is usually eight 440s at 10-K goal pace with a 220 jog after each.

"I am quite capable of running those 440s down close to seventy seconds. But my goal is to prepare myself to race, not to blow myself down before I ever reach the starting line.

"I keep the effort controlled, and usually my first workout is eight times 440 in seventy-nine to eighty seconds per quarter [33:00 10-K pace]. Over a period of three weeks, that effort remains the same—but the times come down to the seventy-five- to seventy-six-second range [31:30 10-K]."

"Then I begin racing. At that point, I drop the intervals. They have served their purpose. I never, during the interval or racing period, do more than one hard session a week.

"At thirty-nine years old, I recently ran a 1:13:40 half-marathon and a 55:05 ten-mile. Both are PRs."

Nearly twenty years into my own LSD era, I'm still learning. What I've primarily learned in recent years is that this is less a training system than a recovery method. For this reason, I'm more inclined to call it "gentle running" than LSD: it gently replaces what the hard work takes away.

Stronge raced better by slowing down her training. That pace itself didn't make her faster in races; the recovery it gave her did. She went into her 10-Ks healthy and eager, with all the speed she needed.

Fulton and Stiller added small amounts of gentle speed to their gentle distance. Fulton sped up twice a week. "On one weekday," he wrote, "I would do form work (six to eight accelerations up a gradual incline of approximately 300 yards). On another day, I would do some relatively easy speedwork (total distance never exceeding four miles) on the track, again with emphasis on form rather than how fast the distance could be covered."

Stiller settled for a single fast day each week. That's all he is willing to do and all he thinks he needs. "Most runners never understood," he said, "that LSD was simply an alternative method of training for those who constantly overworked or injured themselves doing intervals—or simply disliked speedwork."

Speed Games John Salmonson of Honolulu found speed training distasteful. He wrote, "I run seventy-plus miles per week and do fairly well in long races (considering my six-foot-two, 175-pound size): 3:20 PR in the marathon. But I don't like speedwork, and subsequently my 10-K best is only 42:10. How can I get past this dislike/fear of short, hard races and get my time into the 39s?"

"If you don't like speed training," I replied, "don't do it. You obviously do like to race, so *race* yourself into anaerobic sharpness. Temporarily abandon all long racing and most long runs. In their place, race weekly at about half the 10-K distance.

"On weekends when there aren't races available, fake them. Run at or somewhat faster than your ideal 10-K pace, but for a much shorter distance in these tests. The beauty of this faster work is that you don't need to take it very often or for very long to see dramatic results. This is particularly true for those of us who normally shun faster running."

One of the all-time great racers, four-time Olympian George Young, advised sharpening for racing *by* racing; learn to handle the stresses of racing by experiencing the real thing. He called this the most specific, most exciting form of speedwork. The theory is sound, but in practice racing yourself into race shape is impractical and risky: impractical because you seldom find races of just the right distance at just the right time you need them, and risky because the leap from gently paced training to full-speed racing may be too long to make all at once.

Tests overcome both objections. You can schedule them anytime, at any distance, and you can insert them as transition steps between the relative ease of training and extreme effort of racing.

Or you can test for the reason I do: because running fast can be fun. In all my running life, I've never gone more than a few weeks between fast runs. I've never strayed far from racing and race-like testing. I never want to leave behind the sensation of lifted knees, extended strides, pumped arms, and labored breaths. This stopped being training long ago. It is my link to my running past. My first runs were all-out miles, and whenever I run a fast mile now I remember every one that came before. Times change; feelings don't.

My plan is to alternate fast tests one weekend with long ones the next. But I usually choose speed three weeks out of four. Long runs are just more of the same, while fast ones are a radical departure from the norm.

I've tested all sorts of recipes for these tests in recent years: a mile of four quarters with one-lap walks between; a mile with no walking; fifteen minutes of fast running mixed with jogging; fifteen minutes with no breaks. The mixture I now use is most appetizing.

My magic number on speed days is *ten*. The session totals ten laps on a quarter-mile or 400-meter track. I take a total time for the fast parts and later work out an average pace. That pace falls between one and two minutes per mile faster than normal; the faster it is, the more often I walk.

I may run the whole two and one-half miles without a pause, or break it into smaller pieces—miles, half-miles, quarters—with five-minute walks between bursts of speed. A lap of walking takes about five minutes (and, yes, that lap does count toward the total distance).

The decision on the exact mixture rests not on goals but on whims. I never plan what to run until I'm warming up, and sometimes wait to decide until the first fast laps. Half the fun of running fast is letting what happens happen, instead of trying to make the numbers fit a pre-determined plan.

CHAPTER FIFTEEN

Going in Style

On the Ball

"This is my thirtieth consecutive year of racing and training without so much as a two-week layoff," said Tom Osler in 1983. The ultramarathoner and author of the *Serious Runner's Handbook,* defines a "serious" problem as one that slows him even slightly.

"The most serious one I've had to endure has been a sore left heel which I injured after twisting my ankle in 1980," he explained. "This soreness has bothered me off and on ever since. It has never been so bad that it stopped me from running. But it has taken much of the fun from my runs and has caused me to lose interest in ultras."

The analytical Osler (he works as a college math professor) found relief by changing his running form—more specifically, his foot plant. "I switched to a ball-heel-toe foot placement. Like most long-distance runners, I had been a heel-toe lander, and it took me six weeks to grow accustomed to this new foot placement." That was time enough to cure his sore heel.

My experience was similar. Running slowly for the past several years had let me develop some form faults, and an injury had exaggerated them. A heel had bothered me almost constantly for a year when the thought finally struck me that I now ran like an arthritic old man: stiff-legged, flat-footed, short-strided. My feet felt like two clenched fists.

I ran this way to reduce pain, but in the process may have been adding to it. Running was jarring, jamming, and tightening the feet and lower legs. They were acting as ramrods instead of the shock-absorbers they are meant to be.

So I whispered new instructions to myself: "Lift the knees at pushoff, flex the ankles, spring from the big toes, land with the knees slightly bent, fall a little farther forward on the feet."

If a single word can define this style, it is *prance*. Not running like a drum major at a Saturday afternoon football game, but running as if I'm proud of myself. The prancing motion arises from three sources:

- *Foot*. Make full use of it. Land at midfoot, rock back gently onto the heel, then roll forward onto the toes—leaving the ground from the big one.
- *Ankle*. Flex it and snap it. Use it to get bounce from the ground. Think "flex" and "snap" as the ankle does its two jobs.
- *Knee*. Lift it. Pick up the knee and bend it.

This combination led Osler and me back to healthier running as we got up off our heels. We're beyond improving our PRs, but, for you, the more fluid way of moving might translate into faster times.

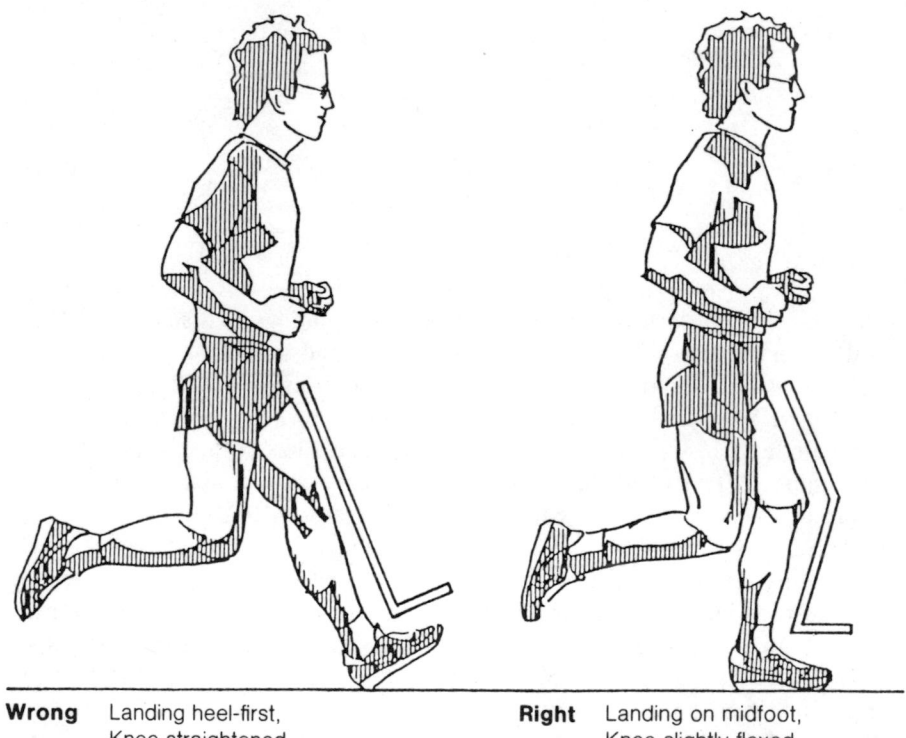

Wrong Landing heel-first,
Knee straightened,
ankle locked

Right Landing on midfoot,
Knee slightly flexed,
ankle unlocked

Figure 15.1 Running Footplant

Ups and Downs Shakespeare never ran a road or cross-country race, as far as we know, but runners everywhere will agree with his lament that hills "draw out the miles and make them wearisome."

Uphill running obviously slows us down, but without giving the usual recovery of slowing. You still may be working at six-minute-per-mile effort while moving at only eight- or nine-minute pace.

Downhill running is easier, but it isn't completely relaxing either. Gravity tugs you out of control. The feet, calves, knees, and thighs take almost twice the beating that they do on the flat.

Hill running has a set of rules all its own. The first word in running uphill is *preserve;* the most important word in running down is *protect.* "Preserving" means not wasting so much energy going uphill that you have no energy left for resuming normal pace when the course flattens. "Protecting" means not letting the downhills pound you so hard that you are not able to run normally when the hill bottoms out. In both cases, get over the hills without getting hurt by them.

Efficient climbing has less to do with technique than attitude. When you run up hills, neither fear them nor fight them; simply adjust to them. If you were riding a bicycle uphill, you would shift into a lower gear. The speed would drop, but you'd pedal with about the same effort. Do the same when you run: maintain a constant workload while ascending, even as the pace naturally declines.

Proper (read: *protective*) downhill running is more difficult than it might first appear, as illustrated by this exchange at a running clinic.

"I do okay on the uphills," one man said. "But the part that should be easy—coming back down—gives me the most trouble. What can I do?"

I offered the standard advice by quoting Kenny Moore, a consummate downhill specialist who once ran a sub-four-minute opening mile on a slope of a 10-K. Moore advised holding the body perpendicular to the surface and letting gravity do the work.

"I know all that," said the questioner. "But have you ever tried running that way down a steep hill? It pounds you to death. What I want to know is how to avoid that."

When I admitted ignorance, another speaker onstage at the clinic came to my rescue. Tom Miller was studying for an exercise-physiology doctorate at the University of Utah, giving particular emphasis to the ways runners move.

"Run like a question mark," said Miller. He explained the enigmatic advice as he assumed the wrong and right positions.

"The natural tendency when running downhill is to reach out with the front leg, lock the knee, and slam down heel-first. You lean backward, arch the back, and possibly throw back the head. That's all wrong. You're braking and taking more shock than you should."

Then Tom demonstrated the question-mark style. "Instead of 'running tall,' as you would on the flat, you 'run short,' as if you're sneaking up behind someone. Keep your feet under you and the footfall as quiet as possible. Bend the knees more than normal. Hold your rear down and slightly protruding. Look at the ground in front of you."

The time to learn about running hills is before the races, in hilly training and tests. Hill racing is strength work, and hill training/testing builds the necessary muscles for it.

According to Dr. Bob Fitts, former national-class road racer and now an exercise physiologist, "Hill training is the foundation upon which all of the other principles of successful hill racing must stand. There is a simple reason for this. When running up a hill, extra muscle fibers are used to perform the extra work. These fibers recruited for hill running are not generally used while running on level terrain." Simply put, untrained muscles fatigue quicker.

Fitts' conclusion: "Train on the hills, and almost any tactic will work. Without hill training, all tactics are doomed to failure."

My conclusion: Choose a test course as nearly identical to the racing course as you can make it.

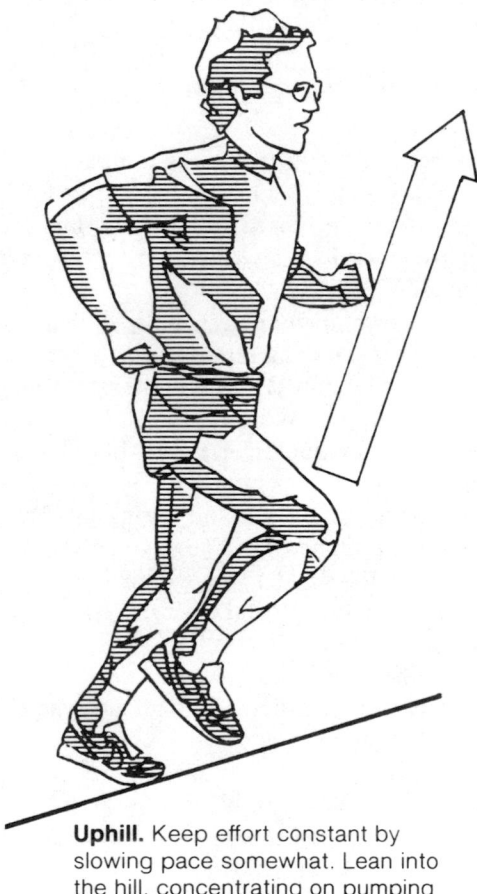

Uphill. Keep effort constant by slowing pace somewhat. Lean into the hill, concentrating on pumping harder with the arms and "lifting" with the knees and ankles.

Figure 15.2 Uphill running

Downhill. Absorb the added shock by keeping center of gravity low and landing with exaggerated flex of knees. Look down to promote a forward lean.

Figure 15.3 Downhill running

CHAPTER SIXTEEN

Almost Like Race Day

Testing Everything

May all your race day surprises be pleasant ones!

The best surprise you can give yourself is to run farther or faster—or both—than you did before. Yet even that type of result shouldn't be too surprising. After all, haven't you trained and tested with that improvement in mind?

Testing means rehearsing in advance the stresses of the race so they won't occur as unpleasant shocks on race day. You test separately at the racing length and at race pace. Long tests (lasting the approximate length of your race but usually run at a slower pace) acquaint you with the feeling of covering the full distance. Fast tests (run at race pace but no more than half the distance) introduce you to the mechanics of moving at full speed. You bring the two factors together in the race itself.

The subject of testing doesn't end with distance and pace. These dress rehearsals serve many other purposes, all designed to immunize the runner against rude surprises. Very little that happens to you on race day should be happening for the first time.

Don't just simulate the race: mimic its whole day. Start the night before the event, by eating and sleeping as you would if you were about to compete, and continue pretending you were racing until you refuel and rest after the test. Pay special attention to five areas:

1. **What to eat and drink.**

   If what you normally do works, don't change it. If you normally eat several hours before running, eat the same items in the same amounts now; if you don't eat before a run, don't start now. If you drink a cup of coffee in the morning, drink that one cup. If you must experiment with items added to or deleted from the pre-event diet, make adjustments before race day. If something seems to help you test better, keep it in the race routine; if it bothers you now, cut it out then.

   When and what you drink during a long race protects your health and affects your performance. Practice drinking during long tests at intervals similar to those in races (generally every two to three miles). What to drink is the subject of some controversy. Some scientists claim that plain water works best, yet runners report good results from taking electrolyte mixtures such as ERG and sugared drinks such as defizzed cola. Again, the most important experiments are your own, and the time for experimenting is during long tests.

2. **What to wear.**

   The cardinal rule: *nothing new on raceday.* This applies most specifically to the single most critical item of equipment: the shoes. The temptation is to run in lighter footwear, thinking that every ounce of weight shed converts into minutes and seconds gained. This may be true in theory. In fact, you're giving up protection while adding greatly to impact stress. Any gains in time might be canceled out by muscle soreness at best, injuries at worst. When adding distance, speed, or both, stick with the shoes you know you can trust. Save the experimentation for everyday training runs. You might find (as noted in Chapter Five) that you can tolerate racing shoes all the time. On the other hand, realize that today's training shoes are lighter than the "racing" flats of a few years ago, so you never need to carry much of a load.

   The "nothing new" rule applies to clothing. Dress for the test exactly as you would for a race. Underdress rather than overdress, keeping in mind that temperatures automatically rise by twenty degrees when you start running. Being comfortable at the starting line means you'll soon feel too warm.

3. **When to test.**

   Most road races, for practical reasons of traffic and temperature, start in early to mid-morning. The hour may present problems if you normally aren't fully awake until noon, or if you don't generally run until sundown. You can't change the starting time, so a personal change is in order on this particular day. If the race starts at 8:00 A.M., test at eight o'clock. Much as this might hurt, get out of bed two hours earlier and perhaps take a shower *before* running to aid in the waking-up process.

You morning runners face a different set of problems on those rare occasions when races are scheduled in the afternoon or evening. You aren't accustomed to waiting all day to run; you aren't used to planning your daytime activities around a run; and, most of all, you aren't adapted to the warmer temperatures of afternoon. Delay your tests until the hour of the race in order to experience all of these conditions and to find ways of coping with them.

4. **Where to test.**

Familiarity breeds confidence. If you know what to expect from a race course, you're more confident that you can run it well. Test yourself on the course itself or on a reasonable facsimile thereof. Match the surface, terrain, and surroundings of race day as closely as possible. Test for road racing on the roads, for cross-country over the country, for track by running track. If the race has hills, practice running up and down slopes of the same steepness and number. Familiarity breeds competence.

5. **What to do before and after.**

A race doesn't start at the starting line, and it doesn't finish at the finishing chute. Neither should a test. The subjects of warming up and cooling down are important enough to fill the second half of this chapter.

Warming and Cooling The hardest, least pleasant effort doesn't come at the end of a run but at the start. Recall how you feel as you take your first steps each day. You're stiff, heavy, uncoordinated. You wonder if you've forgotten how to run and why you're bothering to re-learn the technique. Is this how you want to start a race or test?

Now recall how you feel after fifteen minutes have passed. Sweat is flowing as freely as your strides. The running has taken control of itself, and you're on automatic pilot. Your early doubts about how and why you run are gone. This is the way you want to feel at the starting line.

Spend fifteen minutes warming up. A quarter hour is long enough to loosen up both the legs and the head, but not so long that you squander the energy reserves you'll be needing soon. Keep this time period constant for races and tests of all distances and paces, but vary the routine somewhat as working conditions change.

For instance, when racing or testing at short distances (those lasting less than an hour and run quite fast), add two more elements after the fifteen-minute run: a set of stretching exercises, and striding 100 meters, three to five times, at the pace of the race or test.

Stretching and striding become options at longer distances (those taking longer than an hour to complete and more modest in pace). Take a separate fifteen-minute warm-up before any faster-than-normal effort of this length. However, if your objective is distance and not speed—if the test is gently paced or the race is an extra-long one, such as a marathon—simply warm up during its early miles as you would on a daily run.

Today's ambitious runners typically err on the side of too much warm-up. You see them pacing the streets a half hour to an hour before a 10-K race. This amount of pre-event warming serves no physical purpose: it is merely a reaction to anxiety. Think of how you feel after a normal day's thirty- to sixty-minute run. Do you want to *start* your hard work feeling this way?

Today's runners are just as likely to cool down too little. You see them crossing the finish line, stumbling to a grassy area nearby, and immediately starting the post-event celebration. This is no way to start recovering.

If the warm-up shifts gears between resting and hard work, the cool-down period is a necessary shift from racing to resting. Continued mild activity gradually slows down the racing metabolism, and also acts as a massage to gently work out the soreness and fatigue products generated by the earlier effort. The pattern and pace of recovery are set in the first few minutes after the race or test ends.

A report by J. E. Dimsdale, M.D. and colleagues, appearing in the *Journal of the American Medical Association* (February 3rd, 1984), offers a more sobering reason for cooling down properly. The authors studied ten healthy men, between the ages of twenty-two and thirty-five. They found that levels of two powerful hormones, norepinephrine and epinephrine, increased during exercise and continued to rise afterward. Dr. Dimsdale suggested that the continued rise in these hormones during the post-exercise period may be responsible for irregular heart beats and lack of adequate blood flow to the heart muscle.

"The worst possible strategy for exercise cessation," cautions Dimsdale, "would be to have the patient abruptly stop exercising and stand [still]. The best strategy would be for the work load to be diminished gradually."

The best strategy is to keep moving. Walk for at least fifteen minutes after the racing or testing ends. *Walk.* Some experts will advise you to run easily, but walking will give the same benefits with much less effort—and you've already worked hard enough.

Dr. Jack Rockett, a physician and veteran marathoner from Tennessee, values his post-race walking. "I've found that a walk at the end of a run keeps me from being so tight," explains Dr. Rockett. "Therefore, I need to do less stretching. Also, if I walk a mile or two the same day I run a marathon, I am less sore in the following days."

He has the backing of Tom Osler, who wrote in his *Serious Runner's Handbook:* "After a really hard effort, such as an all-out marathon race, the runner should try to keep his circulation going vigorously for some time. Brisk walking would be an excellent start on the road to recovery."

Osler recommends a brief walk immediately after finishing, then another stroll of up to an hour later that day. "The worst thing you can do," he says, "is stop immediately upon crossing the finish line and stand around talking to friends."

The talk can wait for fifteen minutes; the cool-down can't.

CHAPTER SEVENTEEN

Ten-Kilometer Tests

The Perfect Ten

A case can be made for ten kilometers being the perfect racing distance. Certainly the 10-K is the most popular race: more than half of the events nationwide are the metric equivalent of 6.2 miles, and many of the others are eight kilometers (about five miles) or twelve kilometers (about seven and one-half miles) in distance. The discussion here centers on the "perfect ten," but extends across the range of 8-K to 12-K, because the training, testing, and racing requirements are nearly identical.

The fact that 10,000 meters is a traditional Olympic distance might explain the popularity of this race from the organizers' point of view. However, relatively few runners are aware of that fact, and almost certainly didn't know it when they first ran a 10-K. The primary appeal of the event arises from its close resemblance to everyday running. Training runs typically settle into the half hour to hour range, and almost every runner can finish a 10-K race within that same thirty- to sixty-minute range of times. Therefore, the distance is familiar, and neither too long nor too short.

Only the speed of the races is unique. The challenge of racing the 10-K lies in running that common distance faster than normal, but not so fast as to be reckless or dangerous. This is a true race (as opposed to marathons, which often come to resemble survival marches), and yet it is not a mad dash (such as happens in the mile).

The perfection of the 10-K takes other forms. Testing is simplified to a matter of improving speed, and no more than a weekly fast test is required to prepare for race speeds that aren't excessive. No long tests are needed because most runners go far enough in daily training to handle these distances.

If you enjoy racing, you want to race often. Ten-kilometer races allow this because recovery occurs quickly. Applying the standard formula of one easy day following each racing (see Chapter 29), you can safely run 10-K races as often as seven days apart. Marathon specialists, on the other hand, must limit themselves to about one race a month.

Ten kilometers is a great place for a racer to start, and an equally great stopping place for runners like myself who still like to race but don't care to work too hard at racing. I now enter these races almost exclusively; these are the distances I call "home."

I spent the first eight years of my running life training for and racing on the track. This netted me a 1:55 half mile, a 4:18 mile and a legacy of injuries. I spent the next seven years training for and racing in marathon-like events. This phase of my career allowed me to run unspectacular but satisfying sub-three-hour marathons and to survive runs as long as seventy miles. It also resulted in foot surgery from running too far, too often.

I'm proud of all the times and distances I ran in those fifteen years, and I don't regret any of the suffering that went into them. But those times are past now. I'm finished with that kind of working and wandering—at least as regular routines.

What I wrote many years ago in *Run Farther, Run Faster* (Anderson World Book, 1979) is even more true now: "I've been to the extremes of racing. Small, simple five- to ten-milers are the place I've decided to settle down. If I want to make rare trips out from here again, I'm familiar enough with the other neighborhoods to visit them briefly. But this is home." This home may not be as thrilling as the exotic places I visited at the extremes of pace and distance. But this is a place where I can relax, live comfortably and avoid much of the frenetic effort that very fast and very long travel involve.

I urge other runners to visit the places I have. If nothing else, this makes home look better when they return there to settle down.

The Need for Speed Adding distance is a matter of persistence: simply running more of what you already run daily. Increasing speed is a matter of style, of applying techniques not normally practiced day by day. Running fast is a learned skill, and you learn it by testing at that pace.

Dick Buerkle, a two-time Olympian, says a runner should practice the techniques of speed before worrying about the numbers on a watch. The digital watches on almost every running wrist are two-edged swords. On one hand, they give instant results. On the other, they sometimes tell us more about each run than we may want or need to know. The flickering numbers may blot out more important messages.

Buerkle writes in *Racing South* magazine: "I never use a watch during the first few weeks of speedwork. Instead, I think about knee lift, arm carriage, erect posture—all those things that make up the sweet stride. Time is not something you should be thinking about—at least not at first. Going without a watch was a significant factor in my running 3:54.9 for an indoor mile in 1978. Only in my last few workouts did I use a timepiece."

I apply this lesson during my nostalgic weekly visits to the track. I wear a watch only because I will want to know the results later, and no one else is there to time me. But I don't want to know how fast or slow the test is *until it ends*. I check no splits but concentrate instead, as Buerkle suggests, on the more important matters of running smoothly and strongly.

You might argue that speedwork in any form is distasteful and perhaps even unnecessary. I might have agreed with you once, before I found an unlikely hero in Doug Rennie. We've never met, and he may be surprised to hear his words repeated from this source— "Mr. LSD." I once overstated the case against speedwork because fifteen or twenty years ago training was out of balance in that direction. Now I speak favorably about speed because in recent years the balance has tipped too far toward slow distance.

Rennie argues persuasively for added speedwork. He has set all of his PRs—ranging from a 32:45 10-K to a 2:33:51 marathon—since turning forty, and attributes this improvement largely to his regular speed tests. Writing in *The Running Scene* magazine, he examined and rebutted common excuses for not training fast. To them, I add some of my own.

- *I don't need it.* "Ever run a 10-K race that felt like a fifty-yard dash lasting thirty-seven minutes?" A runner drawn into an unusually fast pace, a minute or more per mile faster than the training rate, feels that he or she is sprinting all the way. A sprint lasting more than a few seconds is no fun.
- *My races are my speedwork.* "If you race every weekend flat-out, and if every race is short and fast, then maybe you can get by with little or no formal speedwork. But how many can nod in affirmation to those ifs?" The races must be frequent and must mimic the pace of the shortest racing distance. Otherwise, speed tests must fill these needs.
- *I'll get injured.* "Running with your head and not just your legs greatly minimizes the risk of injury." Racing fast without a proper speed background maximizes the risk of injury. Testing at race pace eases the shock of an abrupt transition from gently paced training to hard racing.
- *Speedwork hurts.* "True, but so does racing. Speed sessions prepare both mind and body for the rigors endemic to flat-out racing." You most fear the unknown. Racing won't hurt as much if you know what to expect and have experienced it previously in tests.
- *Running on the track is boring.* "Who says you have to run on a track? The important thing is that you create [race-like] stress. How and where you do it doesn't really matter." The tests should match racing conditions, most notably the setting. You need to rehearse at racing speed on the track only if you plan to race there.

Table 17.1 *Testing for a 10-K*

While this is labeled a 10-K program, it applies to a range of short-distance races: those 8-K to 12-K in length and lasting between thirty minutes and an hour for most runners. Because you run that amount regularly in training, your concern in testing is not with distance but with speed. Temporarily eliminate all runs longer than an hour and spend the one big day each week learning to run faster.

This plan is designed to improve your speed during a month of testing and racing. The underlying assumptions are that you have not been racing regularly at distances 10-K and less, and that you have taken no recent speed tests. (If this doesn't describe you, the program in Table 20.3 may better fit your needs.)

The special ingredients here are: (1) testing at 10-K race pace but not more than half the racing distance; and (2) racing faster than 10-K pace at a shorter distance.

Week	Big Day	Other Days
1	5-K test at 10-K race pace	30 to 60 minutes
2	5-K or shorter race	30 to 60 minutes
3	5-K test at 10-K race pace	30 to 60 minutes
4	5-K or shorter race	30 to 60 minutes

Half-Marathon Tests

Making the "Half" Whole

My purpose here is to sell you on the hidden beauties of the half marathon, a perfectly lovely little event that is forced to hide behind an ugly name. I'm already sold on this race, for reasons that soon will become apparent.

I like everything about the half marathon except that name *half marathon.* No other road distance is known as a fraction of another. This is made to sound like a low-rent marathon, a discount item. It is treated as a second-rate event on a two-race program, added as an afterthought for those slackers who won't put out full marathoning effort.

Those who do run the "half" are also victims of its name. They think, "If I ran my half marathon in 1:30, I must now be ready for a three-hour race at the full distance."

No one expects Sebastian Coe to run two more laps at his world-record 800 pace for a 3:23 mile, yet we think a runner should be able to maintain half-marathon pace for another thirteen miles. If that were possible, American half marathon record-holder Paul Cummings would be a 2:03 marathoner instead of a 2:12 man (with, I quickly add, potential to break 2:10 if he concentrated on that event). Joan Benoit, who holds the U.S. women's mark in the half, would be running marathons in the 2:18 range instead of nearly five minutes slower.

The typical conversion formula between the two distances for runners of Cummings' and Benoit's ability is to double the half-marathon time and add at least five minutes to predict marathon capability. But here I am falling into the very trap I wanted to avoid. I, too, am cheapening the half by comparing it to its big brother.

The beauty of the half marathon is that it's a unique event, with its own special training and pacing requirements and its own rewards. Don't sell it short just because it isn't as popular as either the marathon or the 10-K. In my opinion, that very lack of popularity is one of this race's main attractions. Halves don't usually bring out the crowds of either the 10-Ks or the marathons. Very few of these events attract more than a thousand runners, and smallness may become an attraction after you've fought your way through a few mob scenes.

This distance—or more precisely, the range of distances well between fifteen and twenty-five kilometers, races requiring between one and two hours to complete—is the least-tapped source of personal records. These "middle distances" also offer unique experiences that frequently remain unexplored.

If I hadn't already applied the term "perfect race" to the 10-K in Chapter 17, I might have argued the perfection of the half marathon. Perhaps the word "attractive"is suitable. The attractiveness of the middle distances takes many forms, the most significant being that these races combine speed and distance better than the shorter and longer events. Ten-K testing almost exclusively emphasizes speed, while marathon tests lean heavily toward distance. The half marathon requires modest amounts of both elements.

The pace of this race is not so fast that it requires a great deal of special speedwork, as might the events of 10-K and less. Those short races themselves, taken regularly enough, can serve as your speedwork for the half.

By the same token, this distance is not so great that it demands extra-long training runs, as marathons do. Two hours is the most time you ever need to invest, and you can finish a half marathon on much less. This is a welcome change from spending all Saturday morning running and the rest of the weekend semi-comatose from the extreme effort of marathon testing.

Even if you train moderately (averaging thirty to forty-five minutes a day, for instance), no "Wall" is likely to loom between you and the half-marathon finish line. This is truly a *race* and not simply a survival exercise.

When you don't hit a "Wall," you spend much less time recovering. Dr. Jack Scaff, who conducts the popular Honolulu Marathon Clinic, tells the Hawaiian runners that crashing during the race is "an injury, and you need six weeks to recover just as you do for any other injury." By emerging from your half uninjured, you can repeat the distance as soon as two weeks later.

Combining Speed and Distance Another hidden beauty of the half marathon is that no one seems to train seriously and specifically for this event. Even people like Joan Benoit and Paul Cummings set their American records while pointing for something else: Benoit to break her national 10-K mark and Cummings for the New York City Marathon.

Runners of lesser ambition can be half marathoners without sacrificing their normal lives to the gods of speed or distance training. Preparation for a half fits so neatly into what they probably already run that they hardly need to break stride while getting ready for this type of race.

How much of the following describes you? Your typical daily run lasts at least thirty minutes but rarely more than an hour. Every week or two, you take a long run of one to two hours. You race often, mostly in the ten-kilometer range. These races are your only speed-work.

Now let's measure that routine against the accepted requirements of training. The two basic needs are frequent runs, taken somewhat faster than race pace but for a shorter distance, and regular runs of full distance but at a slower pace. (Full distance and full pace mix only during the race.)

If you fit the preceding profile, you typically don't train fast enough for the 10-K or long enough for the marathon. But this combination suits you well for the half. Your short races give the speed you need, your long runs provide the distance, and your everyday running allows full recovery between the harder sessions.

If I've just described you, don't change a thing. Don't make any attempt to "improve" your program or to peak for a certain half-marathon event. You're already trained perfectly for this race.

If, however, you're lacking in one of the basic ingredients, or if you want to adopt a new routine that allows more productive racing over a wider range of distances, consider adopting the following schedule of weekly races and tests. (Run the normal, comfortably paced thirty to sixty minutes on all other days.)

- *Week One:* long test, two hours maximum
- *Week Two:* fast test, one hour maximum
- *Week Three:* race, one to two hours
- *Week Three:* recovery weekend, nothing fast or long.

Inspiration for this program comes from Bill Bowerman. The legendary University of Oregon coach taught, as almost everyone now knows and practices, that good results can only come from mixing hard and easy days. Bowerman's years of experimentation taught him that no runner improved without working hard some of the time, but also that no one improved without taking breaks between bouts of extreme effort.

A lesser-known Bowerman principle involves training by cycles longer than a week. My variation on Bowerman's theme takes hard-easy to the extreme of no more than one day of racing or testing per week as part of a four-week cycle: short and fast first weekend, long and relatively slow the second weekend, race the third weekend, then repeating the cycle. This yields an average of about one hard day in ten, which appears to be a productive yet safe ratio not just for half marathoners but for racers at all distances.

Table 18.1 *Testing for a Half Marathon*

While this program applies specifically to the half marathon, it can be adapted to a range of middle-distance races: those 15-K to 30-K in length and lasting between one and two hours for most runners. These races will be both farther and faster than your normal training efforts, so you must prepare for both the added distance and speed.

The underlying assumptions of this plan are that you have not been racing regularly at these and shorter distances, and have taken no recent tests of race length or pace. (If this doesn't describe you, the program in Table 20.3 may better fit your needs.)

The special ingredients here are: (1) long tests at the projected time of your race but run at normal training pace; and (2) fast tests at race pace but not more than half the racing distance.

Week	Big Day	Other Days
1	test at full H-M race time	30 to 60 minutes
2	10-K test at H-M race pace	30 to 60 minutes
3	test at full H-M race time	30 to 60 minutes
4	10-K test at H-M race pace	30 to 60 minutes

CHAPTER NINETEEN

Marathon Tests

What's in It for You?

On the face of it, running marathons makes no sense. What is a marathon, anyway? Twenty-six miles, 385 yards; forty-two kilometers, 195 meters. The people who devised this race didn't even have the good sense to make it an even distance, in either the mile or the metric system.

What purpose does running a marathon serve? I'm skeptical whenever anyone tells me, "It makes me feel so healthy." Maybe some of the early training makes a runner healthy, but much of the later, more serious training for marathons and the race itself should carry a "Caution: may be hazardous to your health" warning. A podiatrist—a marathoner himself—once told me, "I know without looking at the race schedule if there has been a marathon recently. Starting on Monday morning and continuing the next week or two, my office is filled with the casualties of the race."

We can't be going to these lengths because it makes us feel more alive and energetic, either. The hollow-eyed, glazed stare of a runner in the twenty-sixth-mile, post-collapse-point "survival shuffle" shows this can't be true, as do the finishers who hang limply on each other, too weak to stand alone.

It's unlikely that we run marathons because we like to view the scenery: we're running too hard and with too much concentration to know whether we're passing through a park or the city dump. Anyway, most marathon courses don't go anywhere except back to where they started.

Well, then, do we run marathons for the competition, the chance to be a winner, to earn prizes? Not in the usual meaning of these words. Not one marathoner in a hundred is rewarded for placing well, or runs for that reason, or knows or cares as much about the winner as he or she does about himself or herself.

Perhaps that's the point of marathoning. So many people are running the distance now because it means something to them personally. It's a major athletic goal they can reach with their own sweat—not second-hand from a stadium seat or through a TV screen. Whether the goal has any purpose is irrelevant as long as it has meaning.

Mark Twain once defined play as any activity which has meaning but no purpose. We forget sometimes that marathoning is just play—a sport, a game. We waste too much time trying to find purpose in it and to explain it in purposeful, practical terms.

Maybe it's time to admit that running 26.2 miles is as irrational and illogical as batting a fuzzy ball back and forth across a net, chasing a little white ball across a field, or committing assault and battery between two sets of goal posts. None of these games serves any great purpose, none has any great importance to the survival of humankind, but they all have great meaning to the people involved. That's all we should ask of our play.

Marathoning has whatever meaning we runners, by ourselves and as a group, decide to give it. And we've decided to give it more meaning than any other event in long-distance running—perhaps more than all the other races combined.

The marathon is meaningful because it gives a focus to the sport in general and to individual running careers in particular. This is the only distance above 10,000 meters with a history going back more than a century, with legends of its own, and with an Olympic tradition. It is an "ultimate" toward which an everyday runner can climb.

The first goal of a new marathoner is finishing. And to finish, he or she has to train longer than before. This training is a sneaky way of exposing him or her to other attractions of running that are not so obvious: the positively addicting sensations of runs beyond a half hour; the habit of maintaining a demanding schedule; the temporary stress and ultimate satisfaction of sub-marathon races; the support of a group of long training runs.

Once the ambition of finishing is satisfied, the new goal becomes time: improving one's own best time, running a time which all marathon runners understand and appreciate, achieving a time which has no intrinsic value but as much meaning as we place upon it. Times are important because everyone who runs can have one, and because the prospect of improving that time is a driving force which keeps many marathoners running.

First Marathon The first marathon is a graduation ceremony—a twenty-six-mile, 385-yard victory lap. The most demanding work, the build-up of distances which went on for months or even years, is behind you. If you have trained properly, you need not concern yourself too much with how the race will go; it is all but guaranteed to go well.

"The Wall" that marathoners talk about shouldn't give you any nightmares. Oh, it is a very real part of this event, but not an inevitable part. Your ability has little to do with whether you meet a "Wall" or not. Anyone, from the fastest to the slowest among us, can reach a collapse point, and anyone can avoid it. Those who hit "The Wall" have made mistakes, either in training or in pacing.

You will be well-trained long before marathon day if you follow a preparation plan similar to the one in Table 19.1. Like a student cramming for a final exam, you may think you need to pack in all the work you can in the last week or two. Don't! You draw your ability to finish the marathon from a reservoir of fitness filled gradually over several months. Extra-hard work in the final days does nothing but drain the pool at the worst possible time.

Go into the race well-rested. Allow two full weeks between the longest run and the big event. Run minimum distances during the last week, and perhaps rest completely the final day or two. Save your trained-in strength for when it counts.

There isn't much left to say about the marathon itself. The race almost runs itself. Just stay on course and keep alternating feet until you reach the end. You know by now how to choose a pace that will take you there, because you've rehearsed it dozens of times in practice.

Celebrate for the few hours of the race the good work done over the past few months. They are your reward.

Faster Marathon One of two thoughts occurs to marathoners after a race. If they ran as expected or better, they think, "If I did that well on that little training, think how much faster I'll go if I train harder!" And they up their mileage by fifty percent. If they ran poorly, they think, "I didn't train hard enough; I need more work." And they up their mileage by fifty percent.

We certainly must work hard in order to improve, but we can't tolerate ceaseless pounding. The harder the work on some days, the longer and easier the recovery period must be. The trick is to work hard *selectively.*

Run both more and less when training for a faster marathon—more on the big days and less on the little ones. Don't count miles; measure *efforts.* These come in two types: hard, to prepare you for the distance and speed of the marathon; and easy, to recover from that work.

The schedule in Table 19.2 contains two key features: a weekly test that mimics the stresses of the race, and a full week of recovery in between. Because your goal now is to run the marathon distance at a faster pace, you train for both distance and speed these two months.

Increase the long run until it matches the approximate *time* of your marathon, but run somewhat slower than your projected race pace. In other words, you aren't asked to attempt the full 26.2 miles before race day. A three-hour marathoner, for example, races at just below seven minutes per mile. He or she might train for three hours at *eight-minute* pace, covering about twenty-three miles in that time.

Table 19.1 *Testing for a First Marathon*

While this program applies specifically to the marathon, it can be adapted to a range of long-distance races: those longer than 30-K and lasting more than two hours for most runners. The goal for a first-timer at these distances is completing the race, which probably is more than three times as long as the typical training run. Temporarily eliminate all short- and middle-distance races as well as speed tests during this marathon preparation period, and spend one day each week learning to extend training pace over longer distances.

This plan is designed to increase your maximum distance over three months. The underlying assumption is that you have not regularly gone beyond two hours in races and tests. (If this doesn't describe you, the programs in Table 19.2 and Table 20.3 may better fit your needs.)

The special ingredients here are: (1) tests of two hours and more, taken with a five-minute walking break every half-hour; and (2) tests of about half that amount, taken without walks. Base the length of longer tests on your predicted race time.

Week	Big Day	Other Days
1	two hours with walk breaks	30 to 60 minutes
2	one hour without walks	30 to 60 minutes
3	2:00 to 2:15 with walks	30 to 60 minutes
4	1:00 to 1:15 without walks	30 to 60 minutes
5	2:15 to 2:30 with walks	30 to 60 minutes
6	1:15 to 1:30 without walks	30 to 60 minutes
7	2:30 to 3:00 with walks	30 to 60 minutes
8	1:15 to 1:45 without walks	30 to 60 minutes
9	2:45 to 3:30 with walks	30 to 60 minutes
10	1:30 to 2:00 without walks	30 to 60 minutes
11	3:00 to 4:00 with walks	30 to 60 minutes
12	one hour maximum	30 to 60 minutes
13	marathon race	about 30 minutes

Develop your speed on alternate weekends. Run at your projected race pace, but no more than half the marathon distance. For instance, a marathoner with a three-hour goal would test his or her speed with a half marathon in 1:30.

Do nothing long or hard on the recovery days. In fact, to compensate for the extra work involved in the tests, you may want to do even less on the weekdays than you did before entering this program.

Table 19.2 *Testing for a Faster Marathon*

While this program applies specifically to the marathon, it can be adapted to a range of long-distance races: those longer than 30-K and lasting more than two hours for most runners. You have achieved the goal of finishing a marathon-type event, and now you want to run that distance faster. The emphasis remains on long tests, but you now give more attention to speed.

This program is designed to increase your maximum distance over two months, while keeping in mind the importance of occasional faster runs. The underlying assumption is that you have not regularly gone beyond two hours in races or tests. (If this doesn't describe you, the program in Table 20.3 may better fit your needs.)

The special ingredients here are: (1) distance tests of two hours and more (maximum amount based upon your predicted race time), with five-minute walking breaks available as an optional feature; and (2) speed tests at race pace but not more than half the racing distance.

Week	Big Day	Other Days
1	2:00 to 2:30	30 to 60 minutes
2	10-K test	30 to 60 minutes
3	2:30 to 3:00	30 to 60 minutes
4	15-K test	30 to 60 minutes
5	2:45 to 3:30	30 to 60 minutes
6	half-marathon test	30 to 60 minutes
7	3:00 to 4:00	30 to 60 minutes
8	10-K test	30 to 60 minutes
9	marathon race	about 30 minutes

CHAPTER TWENTY

Your
Testing

Plan your pre-race testing schedule by determining the following information.

1. **Basic training**
Indicate the average length of all your runs from the past month
(in minutes): _____

If you have averaged less than thirty minutes, racing is not recommended. Delay entering any events or attempting any race-like testing until you have increased your daily average to a half hour or more.

If you have averaged more than thirty minutes, your training has prepared you for the testing recommended in this program. Maintain an average of at least thirty minutes per day. You are prepared for testing at about twice the length of your typical training run, unless a longer limit is indicated in part two below.

Indicate the average pace per mile of your daily training from the
past month (not counting races or tests): _____

You are prepared for testing at a pace up to two minutes per mile faster than you typically train, unless a faster limit is indicated in part three.

Table 20.1 *Distance Limits*

"Collapse point" is calculated according to the Ken Young formula: three times the average length of the daily run. Compute that average from at least the past month, dividing the total amount of running by the total number of days (even if you didn't run every day). Stop well short of "collapse," limiting the non-stop runs to twice the time of the average training run.

The test amounts can be extended significantly by inserting a five-minute walking break at least every half hour. Author and ultramarathoner Tom Osler maintains in his *Serious Runner's Handbook* that a runner can travel up to twice as far with the walks as without them. Adjust your figures upward by that amount when taking breaks.

Run at or near normal training pace (one to two minutes per mile slower than current 10-K racing ability). Count the walking breaks toward total time periods.

Daily Average	Safe Limit Non-Stop	"Collapse" Non-Stop	Safe Limit with Walks	"Collapse" with Walks
30 min.	1:00	1:30	2:00	3:00
35 min.	1:10	1:45	2:20	3:30
40 min.	1:20	2:00	2:40	4:00
45 min.	1:30	2:15	3:00	4:30
50 min.	1:40	2:30	3:20	5:00
55 min.	1:50	2:45	3:40	5:30
60 min.	2:00	3:00	4:00	6:00

2. **Distance limit**

Indicate the length of your longest run within the past month (in hours and minutes): _____

This amount represents the longest time you currently are prepared to race. To extend that limit, follow the distance-testing recommendations in Table 20.1.

3. **Speed limit**

Indicate the pace of your fastest run within the past month (in minutes and seconds per mile): _____

This figure represents the fastest pace at which you currently are prepared to race. To extend that limit, follow the speed-testing recommendations in Table 20.2.

Table 20.2 Speed Limits

These speed-testing recommendations are based upon length and pace of daily training runs. Do not exceed *one-half* of the distance that you average in training. Select the normal pace per mile at which you train, then determine how to test. Walking breaks are unnecessary at paces up to one minute per mile faster than training rate, are optional between one and two minutes faster, and are required at two-plus minutes.

Training Pace	Pace without Walk Breaks	Walk Breaks Optional	Walk Breaks Required
6:00	5:00-5:59	4:00-4:59	sub-4:00
6:15	5:15-6:14	4:15-5:15	sub-4:15
6:30	5:30-6:29	4:30-5:29	sub-4:30
6:45	5:45-6:44	4:45-5:44	sub-4:45
7:00	6:00-6:59	5:00-5:59	sub-5:00
7:15	6:15-7:14	5:15-6:14	sub-5:15
7:30	6:30-7:29	5:30-6:29	sub-5:30
7:45	6:45-7:44	5:45-6:44	sub-5:45
8:00	7:00-7:59	6:00-6:59	sub-6:00
8:15	7:15-8:14	6:15-7:14	sub-6:15
8:30	7:30-8:29	6:30-7:29	sub-6:30
8:45	7:45-8:44	6:45-7:44	sub-6:45
9:00	8:00-8:59	7:00-7:59	sub-7:00
9:15	8:15-9:14	7:15-8:14	sub-7:15
9:30	8:30-9:29	7:30-8:29	sub-7:30
9:45	8:45-9:44	7:45-8:44	sub-7:45

4. Race plans

Indicate in kilometers or miles the distance of the race you plan
to run within the next month: _____

Indicate your projected time for the race: _____

Calculate the pace per mile that you intend to run for this distance
(divide time by distance in miles):   _____

If your longest recent test (see part two) equals or exceeds the probable time of the race,
and your fastest recent test (see part three) matches the projected pace of the race, you are
adequately prepared for the upcoming event.

If you have matched or exceeded race pace, but are lacking in distance, attempt a long
test before racing. Run the test at full race time but at a slower pace. If the test is not
successful, reduce the length of your race until you are better prepared.

If you have met the distance requirement but are lacking in speed, attempt a speed test
before racing. Run the test at full race pace for no more than half the racing distance. If
the test is not successful, revise the pacing goal downward or race in a longer (and therefore
slower) event.

If you have met neither the distance nor speed requirement, schedule both long and fast
tests before racing. On the long test, run at your normal training pace for the probable race
time. If the test is not successful, reduce the distance of the race. On the short test, run at
race pace for no more than half the racing distance. If the test is not successful, revise the
pacing goal downward.

5. Race-preparation schedule

Write your own monthly program for tests and races, based upon the answers in parts
one to four above, and on the recommendations contained in Tables 20.1, 20.2 and 20.3.
(Substitute a fast test for the long test in Week One if the race length is shorter than the
average daily training run.)

Week	Type	Distance/time	Pace per mile
1	long test	_____	_____
1	fast test	_____	_____
2	fast test	_____	_____
3	race	_____	_____
4	recovery	no testing or racing this week	

Table 20.3 Plan for the Month

This program is best suited to runners who race regularly over a wide variety of distances. These people are well-grounded in both endurance and speed, and therefore can enter these events with a minimum of special preparation.

The plan is based upon one race a month. Two weekly tests, one long and one fast, precede the event. A weekend of recovery follows the race.

Week	Big Day	Other Days
1	long test, full race time*	30 to 60 minutes
2	fast test, half race length	30 to 60 minutes
3	race	30 to 60 minutes
4	no race or test	30 to 60 minutes

*If the race is to be shorter than the average training run, replace the distance test with another fast one.

RACING

CHAPTER TWENTY-ONE

The Competition

Pain in Perspective

"It's a horrible yet fascinating sight," wrote Sir Arthur Conan Doyle, "this strange struggle between a set purpose and an utterly exhausted frame. He was practically delirious, staggering along like a man in a dream."

In this short description of Doranto Pietri's arduous finish in the 1908 Olympic Marathon, the famous mystery writer and creator of Sherlock Holmes captured the essence of racing. A race puts the runner into the classic confrontation between a willing mind and a weak body. When you push to the limit, this conflict is unavoidable. There comes a point in all distance races when the "set purpose" and the "exhausted frame" do battle, as they did to the extreme in Pietri's case. The body has set limits; the mind determines how closely the runner will approach those limits.

European sports psychologist Miroslav Vanek declares, "Physical effort prevails in training, and psychic effort prevails in competition." Racing involves the hardest physical work you can do, but the emotional experiences of racing override the physical demands. These thoughts and feelings aren't experienced every day in training, and they set up conflicts that aren't a normal part of running. How you deal with these emotions determines the outcome of the race.

Before he or she races, a runner may be consumed by a mixture of anticipation and dread. The race itself involves paradoxical blends of control and recklessness, exhilaration and frustration, fear and courage. Afterward, you experience pain and pleasure, the proportion of each depending on whether or not the race met your expectations.

Racing might be described as organized, self-sought torture. It involves various types and degrees of pain, but the physical and psychic pain are constants before and during the race. The pleasure comes afterward.

"Jogging through the forest is pleasant," points out Kenny Moore, an Olympic marathoner-turned-writer, "as is relaxing by the fire with a glass of gentle Bordeaux and discussing one's travels. Racing is another matter. The front-runner's mind is filled with anguished fearfulness, a panic, which drives him into pain."

In describing Frank Shorter's performance in a Japanese marathon, Moore again refers to that pervasive pain experienced by those who race. "Shorter ran 140 miles per week all fall with consummate nonchalance. A thirty-mile day does not strain his prodigious physical resources. Yet in Fukuoka he [Shorter] said, 'The ordeal is between twenty miles and the finish. My only doubt is that my mind is ready to put my body through that.'

"Exploring the forest is easy," Moore contends. "Exploring the limits of human performance is excruciating."

Shorter agrees: "That's why you have to forget your last marathon before you run another. Your mind can't know what's coming."

Racing looks good from a distance. It's exciting to think ahead to it, pleasant to look back at it. But when you're involved in the immediate preliminaries and the race itself, the reality hits home. By the time you realize how unpleasant it can be, it is too late to turn back. Running away from the pain is not an acceptable alternative; that choice would keep hurting long after the immediate discomfort had vanished.

Ron Clarke, an Australian who held most of the world track records at distances 3000 meters and above during the 1960s, writes about his painful confrontations with himself in his autobiography *The Unforgiving Minute*. "In all my races, I feel some degree of pain. This is not remarkable, because any physical activity in which a person extends himself to the limit causes pain. Sometimes it is an agonizing pain which is scarcely tolerable, and when it comes an athlete has to cope with it as best he can—even if it means deluding himself. I remember in my first marathon the only way I could struggle over the last few miles was from lamp-post to lamp-post, promising myself that each lamp-post would be the last." Clarke concludes that "the pain in a race is caused by complete exhaustion. And the more intense it is, the greater the sense of achievement in overcoming it. Most people succumb to fatigue before they need to, because they have not conditioned their minds to cope with it."

Let me hasten to add, however, that the goal in racing is not to become a masochistic brute who embraces pain. Runners simply learn to live with their specialized discomforts, without developing a fondness for or an immunity to all pain.

Kenny Moore offers an example: "In the summer of 1967, I was included in a group of Oregon runners who were invited to participate in a United States Olympic Committee study of high altitude training and procedures. The price of our three-week vacation in the Rockies was to submit every Friday to a series of tests that measured lactic acid content in our blood.

It seemed strange to our doctors that, while we showed no reluctance to run ourselves into unconsciousness at the end of a hard workout (quite easy to do at 7500 feet), the mention of another session with the needles set us to whining like tormented alley cats."

Moore continues, "The explanation, of course, is that we were used to *our kind* of pain. Over the years, we had developed a familiarity with our bodies that let us know how much of the discomfort of extreme fatigue we could stand. Part of the runner's training consists of pushing back the limits of the mind, of proving to his doubting intellect that [racing] won't reduce him to another cinder on the track. But the needle pain was relatively new and exposed our 'innate toughness' for what it was: a learned specialty. . . . Good [runners] are reputed to possess either great resistance or little sensitivity to pain. Yet I doubt whether runners as a group are any more brave when it comes to sitting in dentist chairs or receiving tetanus boosters than the general populace."

Brian Mitchell, author of *Today's Athlete*, writes about runners and pain from a socio-logical-psychological perspective: "Perhaps one of the biggest mistakes which an observer can make about [racing] is to look upon it as a form of self-immolation. It is doubtful whether a wish for pain, or even for discomfort, characterizes the athlete. He does not look upon himself as a victim brought to the altar of the track to be sacrificed, and does not relish the pain that grows from the latter stages of a race. He distinguishes the pleasure in movement from the inevitable pain which has to be endured. The athlete will not like this pain; rather, he will accept it. . . . He knows if he is to achieve anything competitively, he must take himself through speeds and distances that will be uncomfortable. . . . If the athlete wished to cultivate pain, he would buy himself a bed of nails."

Useful Fears After setting a Boston Marathon record in 1970, Ron Hill commented, "I was worrying like hell all the way. But this is a good thing to develop, you know—this fear. It keeps you moving."

Hill had long since come to grips with fear, recognizing it as a component of competition that could be channeled to work on his behalf. It hadn't always been that way. He recalled how fear had worked against him in the 1964 Olympics.

"When I was in Tokyo," he said, "I was the second fastest man in the world at 10,000 meters and also the second fastest man in the world at the marathon. But the night before the 10,000 I was thinking, 'Tomorrow's the day.' There I was, lying in bed, turning the race over in my mind. And the first thing I thought about when I woke up was, 'Today's the day.' My stomach turned over. I didn't want to get out of bed, but finally I dragged myself out. During the warmup, my legs felt like lead, and I was just dragging them around the track during the race. There was no desire to get into the competition. In fact, the only desire was to get away from it; if somehow I could have gotten out of it, I wouldn't have run at all. I finished a disgusting eighteenth."

Hill immediately set about finding ways to cope with pre-race anxiety. He succeeded to the extent that he won at Boston, won at the Commonwealth Games and European Championships, and set world records. The fear remained, said Hill, but he learned to make it work *for* him instead of against him.

"The fear of running a long race can come from the fact that you know it's going to be physically painful. And unless you're a masochist, nobody likes pain; I certainly don't like it. If you dwell on the painful aspect, it can make you nervous. I've now developed some ways of turning off thoughts of the race, some ways I can step outside myself. I can even talk about the race in terms of what it's going to involve physically, and where the pain is going to come, and what it's going to be like, and how distressing it's going to be—without actually thinking that the guy who's speaking is going to be in that position so many hours hence."

Hill learned some important lessons about pre-race "nerves" that other runners might also find helpful. He realized that, within limits, his condition was normal and even beneficial, but that *fearing the fear* could push him outside the safe limits and hurt his performance. By knowing the signs and symptoms, and accepting them as natural, he was better able to control his anxiety.

Pre-race fear takes many forms: fear of pain, fear of competitors, fear of failure, fear of fear itself. And it goes by several names: "butterflies," "tension," "psyching." Whatever its form, a certain amount of uneasiness is a fact of the racer's life. It may feel unpleasant, but that isn't all bad. This is the mind's way of warming up the body for the big task ahead. Think of your fear as doing you a favor.

CHAPTER TWENTY-TWO

Emotional Experiences

Pre-Race Rituals

The mind becomes capricious as the race approaches. It distorts time and magnifies little, unimportant matters into big, crucial ones. The waiting is the worst. You can't wait to get started; at the same time, you don't know if you want to start—or if you will be able to. The last hours drag unmercifully, and a troubled mind fills them with a month's worth of worrying. Every move, every thought seems to pass under a microscope.

"I've got to get some sleep. How can I run if I can't keep my eyes open?"

"Should I eat this? It might upset my stomach."

"Oh no! My shorts are rubbing! What will this do to my legs after a couple of miles?"

"My left shoe has a flaw. Will my feet survive the race unblistered?"

"Nausea. Could it be the flu?"

"Uh-oh. A twinge in my calf."

"Is that wind I hear? Is the temperature climbing?"

"Look how fit and relaxed all those other people are."

Sportswriter Robert F. Jones went back to relive his glory as a swimmer after fifteen years away from the sport. Instead of glory, he rediscovered long-suppressed feelings of fear and dread that were equal parts of his races. He speaks for all racers when he says, "I looked at my watch when I felt *it* start; just twenty-three minutes after noon on the day of the relay; regular as clockwork, as they say, just like it was in the old days. At first it was only a flicker, a brief preoccupation, a butterfly emerging from its cocoon. I helped it along with some of the old rituals. A few curses, as obscene as I could make them, directed not only against my opponents and my coach, but against myself for letting me get into so grave a confrontation."

Jones notes that "the butterfly grew stronger with every obscenity. I fed it further with a mug of hot, strong tea, so thickly laced with honey you could feel it in your wrist when you stirred. I hadn't shaved or brushed my teeth that day, another of the old rituals. Makes you meaner and tougher, we used to believe. The butterfly began to flap its wings down at the base of my spinal cord, and pretty soon there were a dozen more tickling and flapping at the top of my gut."

Jones uses the right word: *ritual.* Jittery pre-racing runners concoct an odd mixture of science and superstition to both prepare themselves and calm themselves before races. The ritual probably works more to put their mind at ease than to benefit the race.

Tapering down on training and psyching up mentally can have some effect on the race's outcome (although training already has set its limits). Pre-race diet and warm-up can help. The idea is to get to the starting line fit, fresh, and ready to run. If the ritual contributes to these ends, it has served its purpose well. However, the principal intent of pre-race primping is to settle the mind. It is an attempt to grasp onto things familiar before plunging into the unknown.

Race plans serve somewhat the same purpose. The unknown can't be entirely charted or planned, of course, but it is comforting to have a general idea—based on past experiences—of what is going to happen and how you'll react. Once the race starts, the plan is used, modified, or discarded, according to what develops. Looking back later, you probably wouldn't have wanted to know exactly what would happen.

There is no easy way to avoid the worries that arise before races, any more than there is an easy way to get through the race. Deep down, runners probably wouldn't want an easy way out. Racing runners are funny people: they worry about hangnails, tummy aches, and any other minor problems that might prevent them from experiencing the real pains of the race.

Moment of Truth The race is not against other runners, but with oneself. Bruce Kidd won against almost everyone he faced while he was still a teenager, yet he wrote later: "Sport does not have to be so exclusively competitive that all but the most skilled must be discouraged from participating. Sport doesn't have to be unconditionally aggressive, either. Anyone who has been active well knows that man-versus-man is but one form of sports conflict. The athlete must compete against himself and the environment, and these common struggles outweigh the interpersonal struggle almost every time."

The struggle with self and environment becomes increasingly obvious as distances grow, and is most readily apparent in the marathon. Kenny Moore, who ran that distance in 2:11, described his approach to competition: "To be effective over the last six miles, one must harbor some sort of emotional as well as physical reserve. An intensive, highly competitive frame of mind over the early part of the run seems to evaporate after twenty miles, so I prefer to begin in a low-key, sort of yawning-sleepy state of semi-consciousness. I watch the scenery and the other runners with appreciation rather than with any sort of competitive response. I chat with anyone so inclined."

Only later, after the twenty-mile mark, does Moore "try to get enthusiastic about racing. A strong acceleration gives a lift, and I can usually hold a new rhythm to the finish. It's more fun to pass people late in the race when it means something. The last six miles is the stage where I try to honestly use everything I have left. That, of necessity, hurts."

But the key here is that the distance runner is hurting himself or herself, not inflicting pain on someone else. By this point in a long race, he or she may barely notice that anyone else is running. Each runner is fighting a private battle.

Early in his career, Frank Shorter often tied intentionally with Jack Bacheler for first place. This outraged some critics, who charged Shorter and Bacheler with working against the purpose of competition. To this, Frank replied: "Maybe in part our tying is sort of an attempt to thumb our noses at the attitude that it has to be like that—the whole idea that the goal is to trample everyone underfoot, to put on your spikes and run over them. It isn't all or nothing with me. I don't consider coming in second losing; it's just not winning. If you're satisfied with what you've done, you haven't lost."

Make no mistake: Shorter competes hard. One doesn't win Olympic gold medals and run 2:10 marathons without being a competitor. Frank, in common with most racers in his events, simply knows where his main competition lies.

Marty Liquori, once America's top miler, knew this too when he said, "Every race makes you a better man. It's not beating the other guy so much as triumphing over yourself."

After the Race Is Over The race is over, but talk of it lingers on. Post-race discussion seems to vary in direct proportion to the distance covered. The farther runners run, the more they're compelled to talk about it afterward.

Leonard Shecter once remarked in *Look* magazine that "people who live with pain, like boxers and long-distance runners, show very little aggression outside the sports arena."

George Sheehan expressed similar sentiments in *Runner's World:* "It is said that we live together and die alone. Runners live alone and die together. Only after a race does their reserve dissolve. In that common agony after the race, runners can reveal themselves to each other."

After long races, physical lows and emotional highs occur simultaneously. Runners who've gone through the agony alone now wallow in the ecstasy together. Perhaps the best explanation of this reaction comes from Kenny Moore: "Human beings are reluctant to accept meaningless suffering. Families of dead soldiers refuse to believe such sacrifice could be in vain. In that way, the pain in a marathon's closing stages can be so great as to *force* meaning upon the run. [Marathoners] submit to the ordeal not in spite of the pain but because of it."

Moore observes that, after the race, runners "hang stiffly to one another, too exhausted to untie their shoes, and they jabber uncontrollably. The pain has made everything suffered so extraordinarily important that it *has* to be expressed. The cramp that seized your leg coming off the hills at twenty miles must be described in loving, urgent detail, if only to the wall because nobody listens. Later, when you recover, you remember your babbling and the others', and in an embarrassed sort of recognition understand you shared something."

The "high" wears off—maybe in a few hours, maybe a day later. It often leaves a feeling much like a hangover in its wake. You realize you are very tired and very sore, and you may feel more than a little depressed. Strangely enough, the post-race blues may be their worst following your best performances. You wonder then, "Now what do I have to do to top this?"

Ron Clarke experienced these feelings time and again as he repeatedly broke world records. His book, *The Unforgiving Minute*, contains an eloquent description of those letdowns: "It has happened in Melbourne, in London, and in Oslo. In fact, almost every time that I've been fortunate enough to achieve a world record, a peculiar sense of disappointment has engulfed me soon afterward. The shouting and hand-shaking have ceased. The record has been confirmed and announced, and the crowd has drifted home. A man is able to think again, to give himself up entirely to his feelings. And invariably the exhilaration of achievement drains away, leaving the record-holder dejected and profoundly weary."

Clarke noted that "perhaps the experience of a record-holder is not unlike that of a young man who has just celebrated his twenty-first birthday. He has looked forward to the occasion for so long, but after the excitement of the party, the congratulations, and the gifts, he realizes that although he is now officially a man, he doesn't feel any different and that life will go on much the same."

There are new races to run, new standards to meet and to beat.

CHAPTER TWENTY-THREE

Forecasting Times

Five-Percent Formula

Before you plan how to run a faster race, think about how much faster you can run. "Set realistic goals," the running advisors tell us; the quickest way to discourage yourself is to choose a target you can never hit. But what is "realistic"? What do recent times at one distance tell you about your potential results at other distances?

For almost as long as I've been running, I've looked for ways to peer into the future. I've read graphs and formulas telling how to predict times ahead based on times past, from one distance to another. More often than not, the math involved in calculating rates of increase and decrease in pace bogged me down.

I was no better at explaining these systems. After I tried and failed at a running clinic, a man from the audience said, "It really isn't as complicated as you make it. All you need to do is add about twenty seconds per mile each time you double your racing distance."

"Your way sounds better than mine," I admitted. Later, I sat down with pen, paper, and calculator to test the man's theory. The difference in the men's world records—1500 to 3000 meters, 5000 to 10,000, 10-K to 20-K or half marathon, and half to full marathon—averaged sixteen seconds. For the top women, seventeen seconds typically separated the shorter and longer distances.

These are the world's fastest and most durable runners. I present myself as a case study for the average runner. My times typically slow by twenty-two seconds per mile as I double the length of the race. Someone who races more slowly may show a slightly larger gap, perhaps as much as thirty seconds per mile.

While I was trying to refine these calculations, an even simpler formula emerged: The typical slowdown factor at double the distance is a fixed percentage, regardless of your ability. Your time at one distance will always suggest your prospects at another, even when their lengths are many kilometers apart. It is a physiological fact that all runners slow down or speed up progressively and predictably as distances increase or decrease. It is my theory that one's pace typically slows by about five percent as the distance doubles and improves by that amount as the distance drops by half.

For instance, a half marathon is roughly twice the length of a 10-K. Say you run the shorter race at 6:30 mile pace. Add five percent to that, and you can count on running 6:50 miles during your half. A five-minute mile pace (thirty-one minutes) for 10-K predicts 5:15 pace (1:07) for a half marathon and a marathon at 5:30s (2:25). The five-percent formula yields probable times of 1:18 and 2:43 for a thirty-five-minute 10-K runner, 1:29 and 3:07 for one with forty-minute speed, and 1:40 and 3:30 based on forty-five-minute ability.

The formula has values even greater than predicting future results. It serves as an important guideline for pacing the upcoming race and for making changes in race preparation. You can't know in advance exactly how any race will end, but the five-percent formula can give you a better idea how it should *start*. Base your pace plans on the predicted time. (More on this subject in Chapter 24.)

Looking at the formula another way, you should expect about a five-minute improvement in marathon time, and two and one-half minutes in the half marathon for each one-minute drop in 10-K time. This assumes, of course, that you are equally proficient at the three most popular road distances. A runner with highly polished speed but limited endurance will slow by more than five percent as the distance doubles, while one who puts in mega-miles of low quality may run almost the same pace in every race.

Your speedup/slowdown factor probably won't be exactly five percent. Dramatic variations from this figure, however, may signal the need for changes in training. Whatever your slowdown factor is, it should remain fairly constant across the full racing spectrum. You can use this figure to test the effectiveness of your race preparation. If you see less than the expected difference between 10-K and marathon pace, for example, your speed needs attention. If you run a marathon slower than your 10-K time had predicted you should run the longer distance, give extra emphasis to your endurance.

More Formulas While I use the five-percent formula as a basis for time projections in Chapter 25 (races in the 10-K range), Chapter 26 (half-marathon range) and Chapter 27 (marathon range), two other systems of predicting bear mentioning here. The first, summarized in Table 23.1, came from Gerry Purdy of Colorado and his computer. Mike Tymn of Hawaii offered another formula after reading a magazine article of mine.

"Concerning your race predictions," wrote Tymn, "you might consider approaching them this way. Although the marathon is 4.22 times as long as ten kilometers, the average difference between the times of well-conditioned runners is 4.65. For example, a person capable of a 30:00 10-K should be able to run a 2:19:30 marathon [thirty minutes times 4.65 equals 139.5 minutes] if he has a good balance of strength and endurance. Conversely, a runner who can do a three-hour marathon should be able to turn in a 38:42 10-K [188 minutes divided by 4.65 equals 38.6 minutes]."

On the general subject of time predictions, runner-coach Larry Waldman of Pennsylvania issues this warning: "Runners should be advised not to allow formulas to place a limit on how fast they can run. Work and patience can enable the runner to reach goals thought to be unattainable."

Agreed. Formulas such as this can help the runner set realistic goals, and then plan training and pacing accordingly. They can provide road maps for the rather unfamiliar territory of the middle distances. These numbers, however, should not place artificial limits on performance or take the element of surprise out of racing results. Exploring the unknown and unknowable is a major reason to race—at any distance.

Table 23.1 Equal Times

Racing pace slows as distance increases; that much you already know. What you need to learn is the normal rate of slow-down. This helps you set a realistic race goal at an unfamiliar distance, plan a sensible pace, and know whether to feel glad or sad about the result.

Dr. Gerry Purdy, co-author of *Computerized Running Training Programs,* produced a set of equivalent times, from which the following table is adapted. To use this table, find your approximate time at any of the distances, then read across. The corresponding times (all rounded to the nearest minute) indicate your potential in these events, according to Dr. Purdy's calculations.

Note that these marks differ slightly from those in Tables 25.1, 26.1, and 27.1. Decide which formula works best for you.

10-K	15-K	20-K	H-M	25-K	30-K	Mar.
30 m.	46 m.	1:03	1:07	1:21	1:39	2:25
31 m.	48 m.	1:05	1:09	1:23	1:42	2:30
32 m.	49 m.	1:07	1:11	1:25	1:45	2:35
33 m.	50 m.	1:09	1:13	1:28	1:48	2:40
34 m.	52 m.	1:11	1:15	1:31	1:51	2:45
35 m.	53 m.	1:13	1:17	1:34	1:55	2:50
36 m.	55 m.	1:15	1:19	1:36	1:58	2:55
37 m.	57 m.	1:18	1:22	1:39	2:02	3:00

Table 23.1—Continued

10-K	15-K	20-K	H-M	25-K	30-K	Mar.
39 m.	59 m.	1:20	1:24	1:42	2:05	3:05
40 m.	1:00	1:22	1:27	1:45	2:08	3:10
41 m.	1:02	1:24	1:29	1:48	2:12	3:15
43 m.	1:05	1:27	1:32	1:51	2:16	3:20
44 m.	1:07	1:30	1:35	1:54	2:20	3:25
45 m.	1:09	1:33	1:38	1:58	2:24	3:30
47 m.	1:11	1:36	1:41	2:01	2:28	3:35
48 m.	1:13	1:38	1:44	2:04	2:31	3:40
49 m.	1:15	1:41	1:47	2:08	2:35	3:45
50 m.	1:18	1:44	1:50	2:12	2:39	3:50
52 m.	1:20	1:47	1:53	2:15	2:43	3:55
54 m.	1:22	1:50	1:56	2:18	2:47	4:00

CHAPTER TWENTY-FOUR

Pacing
and
Tactics

Your One Competitor

"Survival of the fittest" is the best way to describe most races. The typical pattern is seen most clearly in a mile race on the track. At the end of the first lap, all fifteen runners are bunched within a few yards. At the half-mile point, five of them have dropped off the pace and are slipping back. At three-quarters, five more have fallen away from the front runners. Three more slip behind on the backstretch. Coming off the final turn, two runners remain in contention. The strongest and fastest of the two wins the race.

A good race, you might say. It certainly was—for the leaders who could maintain the pace. But what about the other ten who tried to stay close to the leaders and couldn't? They started too fast, lost contact and momentum, and finished more slowly than if they'd let the front-runners get away at the start.

Dreams of glory and front running are fine—if you have the ability to carry through on them. In any race, however, only a few runners are capable of handling front-running pace. The majority will be hurt by this tactical blunder.

Arthur Lydiard, the renowned coach from New Zealand, advises that most runners "should firmly resist the temptation to go with the local champion for the first half-mile.

The ideal starting pace is the pace he knows he can maintain all the way. Only among top athletes who are fighting for championship honors should it be necessary to adopt this tactic. Between them, fast take-offs in an attempt to break up the field are expected and warranted. But others should be warned not to get tangled up in this sort of cut-throat running, as they are the ones whose throats will be cut first."

A key lesson of the running revolution has been that running is too good to be enjoyed only by the fittest and fastest runners. A lesson in racing from the sport's period of explosive growth has been that personal records are the most valuable prizes in any race. Not everyone can run fast, but anyone can break his or her own record. The way to break records is to ignore the runners out in front and to concentrate on pacing one's own race properly.

Split Decisions Every race is really two races. The parts are about equal size, but they differ dramatically in content.

The first half seems easy—often too easy. You know you should be saving something for later, but your body is pleading, "Faster!" You find it hard to hold back.

Then comes the second half, which is almost a different race. This is where you begin to hurt. Where did all that speed and energy go? Your body now cries, "Slower!" and you know you should be going faster. You find it hard to hold on.

Bad races are the result of a common human failing: running fast when we feel fresh, and slowing when we start to hurt. Good races, on the other hand, are largely the result of ignoring instincts of freshness and pain: holding back when we feel best, and saving energy to spend when we feel worst.

The difference between a good race and a bad race is how well or poorly we hold up in the last part. The first half merely sets the stage; the last half is where the main performance takes place. The strength of the final performance rests on the groundwork that was laid at the start.

The two-sided character of a race demands that the racer approach the event with a split personality. Ideally, you treat the stage-setting half with the coolness, care, and restraint of a technician. There's a definite job to do here, with certain narrow time limits; this is the businesslike part of racing.

In the second half, the race changes style, and the racer adopts a new role to match. Now you are an artist, an actor. You have to perform on the stage that has been set. You dispense with caution and inhibition, and race with creative abandon, with everything you have left. If the technician has done his or her job, the artist can perform well. If not, the mistakes of the first half come back to haunt you in the second.

Enough analogies; let's explore in some detail this concept of two-part racing. Arthur Lydiard has outlined a principle of pacing the mile race which applies to an even greater degree as the racing distance increases. "In my opinion," declares the coach from New Zealand, "the best way to get full benefit of ability in the mile is to go out with the attitude that it is a *half mile* race and, as far as you are concerned, the time to start putting on the pressure is when the first half mile is behind you."

Lydiard wasn't talking so much about a slow start as a *cautious* one. "The ideal starting pace," he maintained, "is the pace [the runner] knows he can maintain all the way." At first, it will seem too easy; later, the same pace will feel nearly impossible to maintain.

The coach, whose athletes have won three Olympic gold medals and held world records from 800 through 5000 meters, adds, "The three and six miles [5-K and 10-K] are far more exacting than the mile, and the athlete has to exercise more caution. It is far easier to go too fast, too soon in the six-mile than in the mile."

This advice is even more sound for races of marathon length. Here, the runner must exercise even more self-control. Early pacing mistakes that would mean a slower finish in a 10-K are likely to yield a non-finish in a marathon.

Lydiard has referred to even-pace running as "the best way to get the best out of yourself." For our purposes, "even pace" means that the times for the two halves of any race are very close to equal. The closer the two halves are to equality, the more efficient the pacing has been. If you start faster than you finish, you lose considerably more speed in the last half than you gained in the first. However, it is also possible to drop so far behind even pace in the early stages that the lost time can never be made up.

The "safety range" for pacing is about five seconds per mile on either side of even pace. For instance, a 12:00 two-miler would want to run between 5:55 and 6:05 for each of the miles.

These figures haven't been pulled from the sky. A review of world records indicates that most of the splits fall within one or two seconds per mile of even pace, and none of them varies by as much as five seconds. If this method applies to the fastest and finest-conditioned runners in the world, it should apply to those of average ability, too. Perhaps attention to pacing is even more critical to the runner with less basic speed, less training background, and far less to gain from bold tactical gambles.

Runners of all abilities can profit by timing at least the halfway split of races, and later analyzing pace. You find the five-seconds-per-mile tolerances by using this formula: subtract the fast half from the slow half, then divide the difference (in seconds) by the distance (in miles).

For example, if a forty-minute 10-K runner's times for the halves are 19:30 and 20:30, he or she slowed down by one minute—or about ten seconds per mile—en route. This slow-down factor is excessive. Next time, for the sake of more economical pacing and a faster overall time, the runner should start no faster than 19:45. (Table 24.1 summarizes the "safety margins" for all the standard racing distances. Chapter 25 gives more specific pacing recommendations for the 10-K, Chapter 26 covers the half marathon, and Chapter 27 advises marathoners on their splits.)

Table 24.1 *Perfect Pacing*

Steady pacing sets records. Start too quickly, and you lose at least two seconds late in the race for every one you thought you'd "put in the bank" in the early miles. Start too slowly, however, and you can't make up all the time you've squandered.

Pacing involves spreading scarce resources evenly over the entire distance. This is done by starting fast enough but not too fast. In practical terms, the two halves of the race should come within about five seconds per mile of equal time.

The "safety margins" below are based upon the five-seconds-per-mile factor. Divide both your racing distance and projected time by two, then add and subtract the appropriate amounts to determine what your fastest and slowest halves should be.

For instance, the distance is 10-K and the time forty minutes. The 5-Ks should be no faster than 19:29 and no slower than 20:31. If the splits fall outside this range, the race was run inefficiently.

Racing Distance	Halves	Safety Margin
8 kilometers	2.5 miles	plus/minus 25 sec.
10 kilometers	3.1 miles	plus/minus 31 sec.
12 kilometers	3.75 miles	plus/minus 38 sec.
15 kilometers	4.15 miles	plus/minus 47 sec.
20 kilometers	6.2 miles	plus/minus 1:02
half-marathon	6.55 miles	plus/minus 1:05
25 kilometers	7.25 miles	plus/minus 1:17
30 kilometers	9.3 miles	plus/minus 1:33
marathon	13.1 miles	plus/minus 2:35

CHAPTER TWENTY-FIVE

Ten-Kilometer Races

Smaller and Better

Bill Rataczak, listen closely to me. The race you direct is minor-league, with little to distinguish it from hundreds of other races like it, held any weekend of the year anywhere in the country. Don't take offense, Bill. I mean this not as a slur but as a high compliment.

Rataczak is an airline pilot. (In the 1970s, he flew the plane hijacked by that notorious air pirate, D. B. Cooper.) Annandale, Minnesota, is where Bill comes home to roost and where he conducts the annual Heart of the Lakes 10-K.

This race and others like it—races unknown outside of their immediate areas—form the base that supports the major-league events. These small races are the invisible bedrock of the sport, but I often forget that. Because of my job, I'm drawn to the bright lights and big crowds of the cities. The mega-races there are the most public face of running in the 1980s. But they aren't running as I first came to know it.

The Boston Marathon drew 200 runners when I started road racing. San Francisco held an annual event for a few dozen people, and it still hadn't been named Bay to Breakers. Peachtree and the New York Marathon were years away from their birth. The term "10-K" hadn't yet been coined.

I ran my first road races in California, in the company of fewer than a hundred fellow escapees from the track. The road sport attracted me because of its family-picnic atmosphere and the chance to make something besides left turns. I enjoyed running through the countryside with companions but away from crowds. I still do, but I'm too busy traveling the major-league circuit to do much racing at the roots of the sport.

The Annandale race isn't the New York Marathon, Bay to Breakers, or Peachtree; but then, it doesn't try to be anything but itself. You won't read any feature stories about it in national magazines, and Rataczak doesn't expect any to appear. His race features no celebrity runners. It pays no prize money.

He invited me to Minnesota not as a reporter but as a friend. I'd never been to Annandale before and knew only the Rataczaks when I arrived in this town, an hour from the Twin Cities. But I instantly felt at home there, because I'd run in dozens of towns and as many events just like this place and race. I felt I was coming home after too long on the road.

This was not a nostalgic return to the racing of yesteryear, and this is not an appeal to break up the big-city races. Running, 1980s style, offers the best of both worlds. We can visit the major leagues once or twice a year to sample the glitter and excitement that this sport didn't offer ten years ago. And then we can come back home to relax at the minor-league races that operate quietly, as they always have and, I hope, always will.

I came home to Annandale and saw there that the racing I remembered most fondly was not a dusty memory. It is alive and flourishing, just as I remembered it: no wait in line to start, country courses to run, good food and talk afterward. Bill Rataczak's event met my requirements for a perfect race in distance and size.

- Large enough so other runners are never out of sight, but small enough so we never bump into each other; large enough to take over the roads from the cars, but small enough so everyone can run right from the gun; large enough to form a post-race party, but small enough for you to find your friends in the crowd.
- Long enough to be a good workout, but short enough to avoid "The Wall"; long enough to race without the speedwork of a miler, but short enough to finish without the distance training of a marathoner; long enough to leave you pleasantly hung over from the effort the next day, but short enough to let you race again the next weekend.

A field of no fewer than a hundred people and no more than a thousand is my perfect size. Ten kilometers, give or take a few, is my perfect distance. Races of this size and distance make a much more comfortable home than either miles or marathons.

Mile races relate no more to what most of us run every day than a casual drive through the country does to a drag race. The mile is less than twenty percent of my usual distance and nearly fifty percent faster than my daily pace. To prepare correctly for a mile, I would have to do regular speedwork and accept its risks.

If I were a marathon specialist, I would have to give up short races in favor of long training runs on weekends for a couple of months before each twenty-six-miler. I would have to give up even more racing while recovering for at least a month after each marathon. If I ran four marathons a year, I would use up the whole twelve months just getting ready for and getting over them, with no time left for any other type of racing.

For someone who doesn't care to suffer daily or to delay gratification, the perfect run and the perfect race both last about ten kilometers.

Table 25.1 Short-Distance Potential

Performance at one distance accurately predicts potential at another. This table compares times for races in the 8-K to 12-K range. Find your most recent result in one of the two most popular racing distances, 10-K or half marathon, then read across to estimate your current ability in the other events. Eight-kilometer pace tends to be about two percent faster than 10-K pace, while the 12-K is run about one percent slower than the 10-K. All times here are rounded to the nearest minute.

If you have run. . . .		*You should expect to run about. . . .*	
10-K	**Half Marathon**	**8-K**	**12-K**
30:00	1:07:00	24:00	37:00
31:00	1:09:00	25:00	38:00
32:00	1:11:00	25:00	39:00
33:00	1:14:00	26:00	40:00
34:00	1:16:00	27:00	41:00
35:00	1:18:00	28:00	43:00
36:00	1:20:00	28:00	44:00
37:00	1:23:00	29:00	45:00
38:00	1:25:00	30:00	46:00
39:00	1:27:00	31:00	48:00
40:00	1:29:00	32:00	49:00
41:00	1:31:00	32:00	50:00
42:00	1:34:00	33:00	51:00
43:00	1:36:00	34:00	53:00
44:00	1:38:00	35:00	54:00

Table 25.1—Continued

If you have run. . . .		You should expect to run about. . . .	
10-K	**Half Marathon**	**8-K**	**12-K**
45:00	1:40:00	36:00	55:00
46:00	1:43:00	36:00	56:00
47:00	1:45:00	37:00	57:00
48:00	1:47:00	38:00	59:00
49:00	1:49:00	39:00	60:00

Table 25.2 Ten-Kilometer Pacing

Talking about even-paced racing is easier than calculating it. The problem is that races combine two measurement systems. While most events are run at metric distances, such as 10-K, splits are often given at *mile* points and pace usually is computed in *per-mile* terms.

This table takes those practices into account. It lists the ideal paces per mile, and the desired splits at both three miles and 5-K (the approximate and exact halfway points). The ranges of times are based upon even pace, minus and plus five seconds per mile. Determine your probable final time, then plan to start no faster or slower than indicated here.

10-K	**Per-Mile**	**3 miles**	**5 kilometers**
30 minutes	4:45-4:55	14:16-14:46	14:44-15:16
31 minutes	4:55-5:05	14:45-15:15	15:14-15:46
32 minutes	5:05-5:15	15:14-15:44	15:44-16:16
33 minutes	5:14-5:24	15:43-16:13	16:14-16:46
34 minutes	5:24-5:34	16:12-16:43	16:44-17:16
35 minutes	5:34-5:44	16:41-17:11	17:14-17:46

Table 25.2—*Continued*

10-K	Per-Mile	3 miles	5 kilometers
36 minutes	5:43-5:53	17:10-17:40	17:44-18:16
37 minutes	5:53-6:03	17:39-18:09	18:14-18:46
38 minutes	6:03-6:13	18:08-18:38	18:44-19:16
39 minutes	6:12-6:22	18:38-19:07	19:14-19:46
40 minutes	6:22-6:32	19:06-19:36	19:44-20:16
41 minutes	6:32-6:42	19:35-20:05	20:14-20:46
42 minutes	6:41-6:51	20:04-20:34	20:44-21:16
43 minutes	6:51-7:01	20:33-21:03	21:14-21:46
44 minutes	7:01-7:11	21:02-21:32	21:44-22:16
45 minutes	7:10-7:20	21:31-22:01	22:14-22:46
46 minutes	7:20-7:30	22:00-22:30	22:44-23:16
47 minutes	7:30-7:40	22:29-22:59	23:14-23:46
48 minutes	7:40-7:50	22:59-23:29	23:44-24:16
49 minutes	7:49-7:59	23:38-23:58	24:14-24:46

Half-Marathon Races

For the Record

I readily admit to a special fondness for the half marathon, partly for the most crass of reasons. This distance has brought my only recent victories against a watch that seems to move faster as the years go by. All but one of my personal records is older than my first child, and Sarah is eleven as I write this. The lone exception to my slowing trend is the half marathon.

A few years ago, I set a personal record of sorts in my first race at this distance, which was rarely run until a few years ago. I bettered a time set a decade earlier en route to a marathon PR. Okay, so the "half" mark was a cheap one; I take whatever comes these days. More recently, I narrowly better that time.

Once in a while, even an over-the-hump racer can get lucky and sneak in a fast race. I can beat the clock and my old self without really trying. I may not push myself as hard in racing and training as I once did, but I compensate with a new economy of effort which comes from staying relaxed, healthy, fresh, and eager. None of these characteristics were present, however, in the hours preceding one half-marathon race.

A record attempt was the farthest thought from my mind on the trip to San Diego. My calves still ached dully from a fast mile three days earlier. I ate my last meal at McDonald's, gulping down a Big Mac and fries while driving to the airport.

The night flight was delayed in Los Angeles for two hours. I finally went to bed at 1:00 A.M. and slept fitfully. When my host knocked on the door at five o'clock, I told him, "Wake me when it's over." He stuck a cup of hot tea in my hand and guided me to his waiting car.

The temperature had already climbed to seventy degrees at race time. I didn't warm up; no need for that on a day like this and for the slow pace I planned to run.

The first mile seemed to take eight minutes, but my watch read just under seven. That turned out to be the slowest of the miles by nearly a minute. I never dared think "PR"; that would have frightened me away from it. I quit looking at my watch and listening for splits, fearing that would jinx me. I just let the right pace come, let old habits take over, and let time take care of itself. It came out a record by a single second.

Cheap as this PR was, I'm proud of it. I wouldn't have spent these paragraphs caressing its details if I weren't proud. It showed me I can still surprise myself with good times now and then, but I can't *want* them. The record was not the result of any special effort on my part, but of a standard routine naturally suited to half-marathon racing.

I've labeled the 10-K the "perfect" race distance. But as noted in Chapter 18, you may be better prepared to run half marathons. I think of myself not as unique among today's runners, but as fairly typical of them. Our regular daily runs cover about forty-five minutes, our races seldom dip below ten kilometers, our fast tests rarely are much faster than six-minute-mile pace, and our long tests don't often extend beyond one and one-half hours.

An honest appraisal of this schedule tells us that only the everyday training is adequate for all purposes. The short races and tests aren't fast or frequent enough for 10-Ks; the long tests aren't nearly long enough for a would-be marathoner. However, this routine suits a half marathoner. An occasional 10-K race gives experience at running about half the half-marathon distance at somewhat faster than its pace. The long runs of ninety minutes almost precisely match the half-marathon racing time.

Of course it isn't the best possible program for improving one's times at this distance. But it is the less inadequate for the "half" than for the two other popular racing events. A runner who doesn't care to run to the extremes of either speed or distance, but still wants his or her racing times to improve, might find happiness in the half marathon.

Table 26.1 *Middle-Distance Potential*

Performance at one distance accurately predicts potential at another. This table compares times for the commonly run 10-K and marathon with those in the 15-K to 25-K range. Find your most recent result at the popular short or long distance, then read across to estimate your current ability in the other events. The marks are based upon the expected five-percent slowdown or speedup in pace as distances are doubled or halved. All times here are rounded to the nearest minute.

If you have run. . . .		*You can expect to run about. . . .*			
10-K	**Marathon**	**15-K**	**20-K**	**H-M**	**25-K**
30 min.	2:20	46 min.	1:03	1:07	1:21
31 min.	2:25	48 min.	1:05	1:09	1:23
32 min.	2:29	49 min.	1:07	1:11	1:26
33 min.	2:34	51 min.	1:09	1:14	1:29
34 min.	2:38	52 min.	1:11	1:16	1:31
35 min.	2:43	54 min.	1:14	1:18	1:34
36 min.	2:48	55 min.	1:16	1:20	1:37
37 min.	2:53	57 min.	1:18	1:23	1:40
38 min.	2:57	58 min.	1:20	1:25	1:42
39 min.	3:02	1:00	1:22	1:27	1:45
40 min.	3:07	1:01	1:24	1:29	1:47
41 min.	3:11	1:03	1:26	1:31	1:50
42 min.	3:16	1:05	1:28	1:34	1:53
43 min.	3:20	1:06	1:30	1:36	1:56
44 min.	3:25	1:08	1:32	1:38	1:58
45 min.	3:30	1:09	1:34	1:40	2:01

Table 26.1—Continued

If you have run. . . .		You can expect to run about. . . .			
10-K	Marathon	15-K	20-K	H-M	25-K
46 min.	3:34	1:11	1:37	1:43	2:04
47 min.	3:39	1:12	1:39	1:45	2:06
48 min.	3:43	1:14	1:41	1:47	2:09
49 min.	3:48	1:15	1:43	1:49	2:12

Table 26.2 Half-Marathon Pacing

Your halfway time is an important indicator of progress, but few half marathons post a timer at the 6.55-mile point. This table takes that oversight into account by listing the desired splits at the common checkpoints of five miles and 10-K. The ranges of times are based upon even pace, minus or plus five seconds per mile. Determine your probable final time, then plan to start no faster or slower than indicated here.

Half Marathon	Per-Mile	5 miles	10 Kilometers
1:10	5:16-5:26	26:19-27:09	32:37-33:39
1:12	5:25-5:35	27:04-27:54	33:34-34:36
1:14	5:34-5:44	27:50-28:40	34:30-35:32
1:16	5:43-5:53	28:10-29:00	35:27-36:29
1:18	5:52-6:02	29:21-30:11	36:24-37:26
1:20	6:01-6:11	30:07-30:57	37:21-38:23
1:22	6:11-6:21	30:53-31:43	38:18-39:20
1:24	6:20-6:30	31:39-32:29	39:14-40:16

Table 26.2—Continued

Half Marathon	Per-Mile	5 miles	10 Kilometers
1:26	6:29-6:39	32:24-33:14	40:11-41:13
1:28	6:38-6:48	33:10-34:00	41:08-42:10
1:30	6:47-6:57	33:56-34:46	42:05-43:07
1:32	6:57-7:07	34:42-35:32	43:02-44:04
1:34	7:06-7:16	35:28-36:18	43:58-45:00
1:36	7:15-7:25	36:13-37:03	44:55-45:57
1:38	7:24-7:34	36:59-37:49	45:52-46:54
1:40	7:33-7:43	37:45-38:35	46:49-47:51
1:42	7:42-7:52	38:31-39:21	47:46-48:48
1:44	7:51-8:01	39:17-40:07	48:42-49:44
1:46	8:00-8:10	40:02-40:52	49:39-50:41
1:48	8:10-8:20	40:48-41:38	50:36-51:38

Marathon Races

Race Against Time

Marathoning attracts both survivors and racers. The distinction between the two groups is important because it determines how they approach the event. Marathon survivors mainly want to complete the course, no matter how long it takes them. Marathon *racers* want to improve, and their times are the measure of that improvement.

Most runners first enter marathons as survivors, and only after the first marathon is behind them do they wonder, "How can I go faster?" When they ask that question, they have become racers. Later, they will ask, "How much faster can I go?" and finally, "Why can't I run any faster?"

This particular marathon happened to be in my home town of Eugene, Oregon, but it might have been anywhere. The emotions etched on the faces of the Nike-OTC marathoners were universal.

I enjoy watching a marathon in which I know many of the runners and can cheer them by name as they pass, sharing in a small way in their race well-run. And I hate seeing friends reduced to the post-"Wall" staggers in the late miles, when I'm unable to offer appropriate words of comfort.

I prefer to watch marathons a few miles from the finish, where my friends are wearing their most honest expressions—not the relaxed looks of the early miles or the relief of the final yards. Three faces come to mind from the Nike-OTC race.

One woman was near tears as she shuffled past and choked out the words, ". . . not my day." A man still moved well, but his shrug told me that he wasn't doing as well as he'd hoped. Another woman shouted, "I'm going to do it, really going to do it!" These reactions had nothing to do with place in the race. The last runner felt the happiest, the slightly disappointed one was fastest, and the devastated one finished between the other two.

All three runners measured themselves against their personal standards and not by the overall standards of marathoning. The watch gave each runner a chance to feel like a winner. But it also set a higher standard by which they could lose; simply finishing was no longer victory enough. All three had set out to improve their times, and only one did so.

This numbers game is both exciting and risky. Let's say you are new to this sport, and still have most of your improvement ahead of you. You ran your first marathon conservatively, trying only to survive it. Now you have a baseline PR that begs to be broken. This means you are no longer merely running the marathon: you now must *race* it.

Chasing a time adds excitement to your running. You'll probably break your marathon record several times, and each challenge will be replaced by a new and greater one. Each improvement will more satisfying than the last because of the extra effort involved. Be warned, however, that by trying to improve your time you are entering a race you ultimately must lose. The faster you go, the faster you *want* to go; the faster you think you *must* go. No one keeps going faster indefinitely.

In the early 1970s, John Loeschhorn ranked among the country's best cross-country and ten-kilometer runners. He ran his fastest marathon time in 1973, and decided he would let that PR stand forever. "Forever" ended as he approached age forty. Loeschhorn's goal in year leading up to that birthday was to run faster than ever before, and he narrowly missed that old mark six times in seven months.

"Maybe this is enough to expect from a man of my age and talent," he said after the sixth race. "But the greatest fault of racing is that it tends to make us unsatisfied with everything we have ever accomplished and impatient for better future results. Naturally, 'better' is defined as *faster*. This leaves many of us who race feeling forever unfulfilled."

He concluded on a happier note: "I'll be forty soon. Then I'll create a new set of PRs in Masters [ages forty and up] competition and start the foolish game all over again. You'd think that at my age I would be smarter, wouldn't you?"

Table 27.1 Long-Distance Potential

Performance at one distance accurately predicts potential at another. This table compares times for the commonly run 10-K and half marathon with those of the 30-K and marathon. Find your most recent result at one of those popular shorter distances, then read across to estimate your current ability in the longer events. The marks are based upon the expected five-percent slow-down in pace as distances are doubled. All times here are rounded to the nearest minute.

If you have run. . . .   *You should expect to run about. . . .*

10-K	Half-Marathon	30-K	Marathon
30 min.	1:07	1:37	2:20
31 min.	1:09	1:41	2:25
32 min.	1:11	1:44	2:29
33 min.	1:14	1:47	2:34
34 min.	1:16	1:50	2:38
35 min.	1:18	1:54	2:43
36 min.	1:20	1:57	2:48
37 min.	1:23	2:00	2:53
38 min.	1:25	2:03	2:57
39 min.	1:27	2:06	3:02
40 min.	1:29	2:10	3:07
41 min.	1:31	2:13	3:11
42 min.	1:34	2:16	3:16
43 min.	1:36	2:20	3:20
44 min.	1:38	2:23	3:25
45 min.	1:40	2:26	3:30

Table 27.1—Continued

| If you have run. . . . | | You should expect to run about. . . . | |
10-K	Half-Marathon	30-K	Marathon
46 min.	1:43	2:29	3:34
47 min.	1:45	2:32	3:39
48 min.	1:47	2:36	3:43
49 min.	1:49	2:39	3:48

Table 27.2 Marathon Pacing

In no other race is a controlled early pace more critical than in a marathon. "The Wall" awaits those runners who start too fast. (Starting too slowly is seldom a problem with marathoners.) This table lists the desired splits at the common checkpoints of ten miles and half marathon. The ranges of times are based upon even pace, minus or plus five seconds per mile. Determine your probable final time, then plan to start no faster or slower than indicated here.

Marathon	Per-Mile	10 miles	Half marathon
2:30	5:39-5:40	56:25-58:05	1:13:55-1:16:05
2:35	5:50-6:00	58:20-1:00:00	1:16:25-1:18:35
2:40	6:01-6:11	1:00:14-1:01:54	1:18:55-1:21:05
2:45	6:13-6:23	1:02:09-1:03:49	1:21:25-1:23:35
2:50	6:24-6:34	1:04:03-1:05:43	1:23:55-1:26:05
2:55	6:35-6:45	1:05:58-1:07:38	1:26:25-1:28:35
3:00	6:47-6:57	1:07:52-1:09:32	1:28:55-1:31:05

Table 27.2—*Continued*

Marathon	Per-Mile	10 miles	Half marathon
3:05	6:59-7:09	1:09:47-1:11:27	1:31:25-1:33:35
3:10	7:10-7:20	1:11:41-1:13:21	1:34:55-1:36:05
3:15	7:22-7:32	1:13:36-1:15:16	1:36:25-1:38:35
3:20	7:33-7:43	1:15:30-1:17:10	1:38:55-1:41:05
3:25	7:44-7:54	1:17:25-1:19:05	1:41:25-1:43:35
3:30	7:56-8:06	1:19:19-1:20:59	1:43:55-1:46:05
3:35	8:07-8:17	1:21:14-1:22:54	1:46:25-1:48:35
3:40	8:19-8:29	1:23:08-1:24:48	1:48:55-1:51:05
3:45	8:30-8:40	1:25:03-1:26:43	1:51:25-1:53:35
3:50	8:42-8:52	1:26:57-1:28:37	1:53:55-1:56:05
3:55	3:53-9:03	1:28:52-1:30:32	1:56:25-1:58:35

Your Racing

Plan your racing pace and tactics by determining the following information.

1. **Race description**
   Indicate in miles or kilometers the distance of the race: _____

   Indicate your time goal: _____

   Calculate the pace per mile required to achieve this goal (divide time by distance in miles): _____

   Indicate the average length of your daily runs during the past month (in minutes): _____

   Calculate the difference in length between this race and the average training run (time longer or shorter): _____

   Indicate your longest race or test within the past month (in hours and minutes): _____

   Calculate the difference in length between this race and the longest recent race or test (time longer or shorter): _____

Indicate the average pace per mile of your daily runs during the past month: _____

Calculate the difference in pace per mile between this race and the average training run (time faster or slower): _____

Indicate your fastest race or test within the past month (pace per mile): _____

Calculate the difference in pace per mile between this race and the fastest recent race or test (time faster or slower): _____

You should have tested yourself at least once at the full time of the race (but at a slower pace), and at least once at the race's full pace (but at a shorter distance).

2. **Personal record**

Indicate the best time you have run at this racing distance: _____

Calculate the pace per mile of your record time (divide distance in miles by time): _____

Indicate your projected pace per mile in the current race (from part one above): _____

Calculate the difference between your projected pace for this race and your record pace (faster or slower): _____

The most important numbers in any race are those comparing your past and present abilities.

3. **Time projection**

Describe your most recent race performance.

Distance (in kilometers or miles): _____

Time: _____

Pace per mile (divide time by distance in miles): _____

If you are racing at the same distance after no major changes in training, and if the weather and course conditions are similar, the times in the last race and this one should be comparable.

If you are racing at a different distance, refer to tables in earlier chapters for comparable times. Table 25.1 lists short distances (8-K, 10-K and 12-K). Table 26.1 lists middle distances (15-K, 20-K, half-marathon and 25-K). Table 27.1 lists long distances (30-K and marathon).

Indicate your projected race time (based upon the appropriate table): _____

Calculate your projected race pace per mile (divide time by distance in miles): _____

Your actual race time probably will fall somewhere between your goal (in part one above) and the projection from the table. Select a realistic figure as a basis for outlining a pacing plan.

4. Pacing advice

Calculate the splits at key checkpoints if you run the recommended way, at an even pace (multiply pace per mile by the distance at the checkpoint in question):

Distance	Time
_____	_____
_____	_____
_____	_____
_____	_____
_____	_____

The most important checkpoint in any race lies at or near halfway. Calculate your ideal halfway time.

Halfway distance (divide length of race by two): _____

Half of total projected time (from part three above): _____

Average pace per mile to achieve the projected time (from part three above): _____

Fastest starting pace (subtract five seconds per mile from average pace): _____

Fastest halfway time (multiply maximum starting pace by half-way distance): _____

Slowest starting pace (add five seconds per mile to average pace): _____

Slowest halfway time (multiply minimum starting pace by half-way distance): _____

Tables in earlier chapters give recommended paces for the three most popular racing distances. Table 25.2 lists the 10-K, Table 26.2 lists the half-marathon, and Table 27.2 lists the marathon.

CHAPTER TWENTY-NINE

The Aftermath

Recovery Periods

There *is* life after racing, even though you may not think so in the days and weeks afterward. Once you've thought and talked the race to death, once the euphoria has worn off, the post-marathon blues are sure to follow.

We're not talking about post-race pains. You expect stiffness in the thighs and calves, and you wear your limp like a badge of courage. What you weren't prepared to deal with was the subtle destruction: the lingering deadness in your legs, yes, but an even more devastating deadness of spirit. You don't feel like running.

This effect is partly physiological, partly psychological. The goal that pulled you up the mountain for months is gone now, and nothing new has yet replaced it. Some loss of enthusiasm is inevitable. The psyche will heal along with the body, however, if you give them time. This takes more time than most runners imagine, and the worst mistake you can make now is to rush that natural timetable.

You'd be wrong to think that you were well again once the muscle soreness disappeared a few days after the marathon. You'd be begging for trouble by forcing yourself back into full training and racing before your energy debt has been repaid. Too many runners limp into doctors' offices a week or two after a hard race and complain, "I had no problems in the event itself, then this happened in yesterday's long run. What bad luck!"

Luck had nothing to do with it. Heaping abuse upon an already battered body yielded this predictable result. Distance racing is as destructive as it is exciting. Don't miss the excitement, but take extreme care in handling the destruction. Recover from the race as if it were an injury that takes time to heal.

Racing is like a vaccine. The right dose can make you faster than you've ever been before, but too much of it can hurt. Racing is the most common cause of injuries and poor performances. More precisely, *over-racing* is the cause: racing too often without enough recovery and rebuilding time in between.

Two innovative coaches on different sides of the world, Arthur Lydiard of New Zealand and Ernst van Aaken of Germany, hint at how often a person can race. Lydiard says hard speedwork should amount no more than ten percent of one's running. Van Aaken goes even lower; he limited racing and testing to five percent of total.

Using these formulas, a runner is limited to one racing mile in ten. And if you take frequent speed or distance tests, the amount of racing should be much less.

One method of insuring that races are spaced properly is to multiply the race distance or time by ten, then not race again until you've put in that much easy recovery running. This formula automatically lets you race more often at shorter, less taxing distances, and less frequently at longer, tougher ones.

Jack Foster, who has survived into his 50s as a top-level runner, offers an even simpler rule for clearing away the debris of the race. The New Zealander says he won't allow himself to run hard again until one day has passed for every mile of the race. (The race-spacing recommendations in Table 29.1 are based on Foster's formula.)

A Case of Over-racing After fifteen years of almost continuous racing and training, Lee Dorsey has learned much about running, and has lost most of his illusions about himself as a runner. He knows his long history in racing is unspectacular, that he has even less to brag about now, and that the future doesn't promise significantly better results than he has already achieved. But Dorsey also knows exactly where he has been, where he is, and where he is going. We should all be so lucky.

The Californian is a statistician by profession, and his running records reflect the same care that he applies to his job. Every workout, every race time and place, every split is committed to computer disks, awaiting the type of analysis that Dorsey eagerly gives these numbers.

Lee approaches his running as a rational scientist, with one significant exception. He has a blind spot when it comes to racing: he can't resist competition. He has raced more than 500 times, at distances as short as 100 yards and as long as 100 kilometers. For several years, he averaged a race a week, year-round. This racing mania caused Dorsey no end of trouble, and his legs still bear the scars of overindulgence.

"Pain burned one lesson into me right from the start," he recalls. "As a freshman in high school who had been running a slow mile each day for two weeks, I figured I was ready to win a mile race. My dreams came down hard. I started too fast and dropped out, exhausted, in the second lap."

Table 29.1 *Recovery Running*

A leading cause of chronic fatigue, injury, and illness among runners is incomplete recovery from race-like efforts. As a rule of thumb, allow at least one week or one day per racing mile, whichever is longer, to recover from all races and most tests. The recommendations in this table are based upon that rule. Run nothing unusually long or fast during the recovery period.

Race Length	Minimum Recovery
8 kilometers	one week
10 kilometers	one week
15 kilometers	two weeks
20 kilometers	two weeks
half-marathon	two weeks
25 kilometers	three weeks
30 kilometers	three weeks
marathon	four weeks

He learned in his first race how destructive an imprudent pace *during* a race can be. Only after running about 500 more races did he realize the value of pacing *between* races. Starting them too often can hurt even more than starting them too fast.

"What I'm talking about," says Dorsey, "is not recovering enough between races." He explains by pointing to a computer printout. "The last two years contrast sharply. The first year was my best ever. I set a personal record almost every time I ran. But then I went on an incredible year-long racing binge, often racing twice on a single weekend. I was injured or ill much of the time, and my racing results were disappointing."

Only after a knee injury stopped him completely did Dorsey review his old running literature. "I noticed Arthur Lydiard said that no more than ten percent of running should be at racing pace. Tom Osler called over-racing a form of 'self-abuse.' My recent medical history told me I was definitely abusing myself, so I sat down at the computer and figured my racing percentages to see if they correlated with my troubles."

One column of Lee's printout lists his total mileage. He averaged 200 miles a month during these four years, an amount that remained constant until the major injury.

The next column lists the number of racing miles. He did no speedwork outside of races, figuring he didn't need any when he raced so often. During the good year, he totaled seventeen racing miles a month; during the bad year, forty-two.

The third column lists percentages of racing. Dorsey raced about eight percent of his miles the first year, twenty-one percent the second year. "The unavoidable conclusion," he says, "is that I raced best when I raced least, or less than ten percent of my total mileage, anyway. When I went far above that limit, I first undermined my racing ability, then my health. I strive for quality in races now, not quantity."

Plan for All Seasons A runner can't sow and reap at the same time, which is another way of saying that the time for building up between races must far exceed the time spent tearing down during them. You now know this to be true from race to race, but the principle might also apply to seasons of the year. We may need to follow each season of heavy racing with an extended period of recovery and rebuilding.

Arthur Lydiard says a racer can hold peak form "for three or four months" before taking time off from racing. Tom Osler has reached the same conclusion independently. He writes, "One can rarely maintain a high performance level for more than three months."

Osler observes that he passes through cycles lasting about six months, each cycle including one high and one low period roughly corresponding to the seasons of the year. He finds he races best during the "highs" and prefers to run casually during the "lows."

"The six-month performance cycle is of importance to the runner for several reasons," writes Osler. "For one, it allows him to predict which times of the year he will perform best. Likewise, it allows him to determine when he should take a less serious attitude toward racing. Harder, shorter, faster runs can be tolerated during the peak phase and can produce dramatically improved racing performances. Easier, slower, longer training runs are best during the low phase."

Osler's advice grows more relevant as races spread throughout the year and there no longer is any off-season to the racing schedule. The pattern to adopt is alternating seasons of highs and lows (for instance, spring and autumn high, to take advantage of the best weather; summer and winter low, when conditions are least attractive for racing). The pattern to avoid is putting two or more serious racing seasons back to back.

CHAPTER THIRTY

Your Reviewing and Recovering

Review your race and plan for future racing by determining the following information.

1. **Time analysis**
   Indicate your race distance (in kilometers or miles): _____

   Indicate your race time: _____

   Calculate your race pace per mile (divide time by distance in miles): _____

   Indicate your previous best time (personal record) at this distance: _____

   Compare the result from this race with your previous best (amount faster or slower): _____

2. **Projection analysis**
   Indicate your projected time for this race (from Chapter 28): _____

   Calculate the amount by which you missed the projection (faster or slower): _____

A time faster than the projection indicates that you underestimated your potential; aim higher in your next race. It also suggests that your times at other distances (those upon which this prediction was based) are due for improvement.

A time slower than the projection generally means that you have trained inadequately, paced yourself improperly or both. Make the necessary corrections before and during your next race (see Chapters 20 and 28).

3. **Pace analysis**

Indicate your time for the first half of the race (estimate, if necessary, based on nearby splits): _____

Distance of the first half (in miles): _____

Calculate your pace per mile in the first half (divide time by distance in miles): _____

Time for the second half (subtract time for first half from total time): _____

Calculate your pace per mile in the second half (divide time by distance in miles): _____

Difference in pace per mile between first half and second half (subtract lower from higher figure): _____

The difference between first-half and second-half pace should not exceed ten seconds per mile (five seconds either side of even pace). If you ran within this range, you paced the race efficiently. If you slowed down by more than ten seconds per mile in the second half, you started too fast and lost more time later on. If you sped up more than ten seconds per mile, you lost more time early than you could make up at the end. Make the necessary correction in your next race (see Chapter 24).

4. **Place analysis**

Indicate your placings in this race (estimate if necessary).

Overall placing: _____

Total number of entrants: _____

Placing for your sex: _____

Number in this category: _____

Placing in your age-group: _____

Number in this category: _____

A percentage ranking gives a realistic picture of how you placed in comparison with other runners in races and divisions of varying sizes. Calculate those percentages as directed here.

Overall finish (divide your place by total number of starters):   _____

Female or male finish (divide your place in this category by its number of starters):   _____

Age-group finish (divide your place in this category by its number of starters):   _____

5. **Recovery advice**

Indicate the distance of the race in miles: _____

Calculate your recommended number of recovery days (one day for each mile of the race):   _____

Determine your minimum recovery period in weeks (divide number of days above by seven, then round up to next higher full week):   _____

Avoid further races or tests until this number of weeks has passed, but continue normal training during this period. An additional recovery guideline: The amount of racing and testing during any month should not exceed ten percent of your total running time.

Epilogue

"*I*'m in my forties and still want to improve my racing performances," said the man in the pre-race seminar audience. "Am I too old to be thinking about that?"

"Calendar age means little," I told him. "What counts is running age, how long and how much you've run. After twenty-six years and 50,000 miles, I am quite old in the ways that really matter: the amount of running time and mileage I've put on my legs. You and I might have been born the same year, but you're still an infant if you've only recently begun to run. You probably can look forward to many years of improvement."

Dr. Joan Ullyot, author of *Women's Running* (Anderson World Books, 1976) wrote the Rule of Ten which appears to be quite sound as rules of thumb go: "You won't reach your full potential as an athlete until you have trained for about ten years." Runners adapt slowly and steadily to the stresses of racing, she says, and improvement usually continues for years on even modest amounts of consistent training. The beauty of this rule is that the ten-year clock doesn't begin ticking until the runner begins competing. A fifty-year-old runner is promised just as much improvement as a fifteen-year-old.

The rule was valid in my case. I started racing at fourteen, and the PRs didn't plateau out until my mid-twenties. I didn't suddenly fall apart then, like a car whose warranty had expired. I just found I was no longer interested in working harder and harder for smaller and smaller gains.

Jack Foster began competing much later and at a far higher level, but his timetable was similar. He ran a 2:11 marathon—still the fastest ever for a man his age—in his forty-second year. Then the New Zealander found that his devotion to hard training waned.

Foster, who now runs marathons ten minutes slower than he did at his best, speaks philosophically of the slowdown: "The dropoff in racing performances with age manifests itself only on timekeepers' stopwatches. The running action, the breathing, and the other experiences of racing all feel the same. Only the watch shows otherwise."

Times change; feelings don't. Everyone's times eventually slow, but the effort and excitement of racing can remain constant throughout your competitive lifetime if you don't pay too much attention to the watch.

If I don't look at the stopwatch, racing feels just like it did during my first trips around the track in 1958. The anticipation and dread beforehand, strength and strain during, and pride and relief afterward haven't changed—except now I'm visiting old friends instead of making new ones.

Dr. Peter Wood has run and raced longer than I have. He wrote about a feeling of continuity in his book, *Run for Health:* "Some of us can trace a direct line of descent, through running, to our youth. To run is to relive the exhilarating experience of running free that we first enjoyed as children."

"For some runners," Dr. Wood continued, "there is clearly a thin, continuous thread of running, linking many different phases of their lives." He tells of his thread, which extends back to wartime London.

"I first ran a mile at fifteen years of age, in 1944—four laps on a grass track in England. I still have precisely the same feelings of fatigue and excitement when I run a mile today. In fact, I can almost hear the flying bombs rumbling away in the distance as they did on that first day."

My thread doesn't reach back as far as Wood's in distance or time. But this year is far enough from 1958, and Oregon far enough from Iowa, to make me proud that I've kept unbroken the link between then and now, there and here. When I race, I remember all the good times that have come before: the ones on the watch, yes, but the even more important ones that can't be measured.

A generation has passed since I became a runner. I've gone from boyhood to young manhood to middle age. I've been a high school and college student, a reluctant soldier, a newspaper and magazine editor, a free-roaming writer. I've lived in five different states in three different regions of the country, and I've traveled just about everywhere. I've gone from living with my parents to having a family of my own. I've gone from attending track meets with my father to taking my own children to road races. I've gone from slow miler training easily, to fast miler training hard, to modestly fast marathoner training slowly, to slow marathoner and slow miler who doesn't think of running as "training."

Times and places change, youth fades, awards tarnish, old records gather dust. What stays constant and true through all the years and all the changes is the effort and enthusiasm that go into each new run and race.

Your Record-Keeping

You were told at the beginning that this was to be as much your book as mine. I write the guidelines; you bring them to life through your own efforts. The words here are mine, but the theories mean nothing until you put them into practice.

Your writing should have picked up where mine left off. You should be keeping records of your training, testing, and racing results. A daily log—which can be as simple as a notation on a calendar or as serious as a computer program—serves two important purposes: one personal and one practical.

On the first level, the log gives a feeling of substance and permanence to efforts that otherwise would remain as invisible and temporary as footprints on a hard road. You feel a growing sense of accomplishment as the records for past runs accumulate, knowing that you put every minute and mile onto those pages. Each number tells a story worth remembering.

The practical value of the log is that its numbers lend themselves to analysis. Rather than trusting hazy memories of what might have led to high and low periods in your running, you can find your answers by reviewing accumulated facts. As training, testing, and racing data pile up, the numbers form patterns which tell the story of how well or how poorly you respond to your running.

I've been a diary-keeper since 1959. My daily entries are now made mostly to satisfy creative urges, yet the diary has taught me most of my practical lessons. From the day-by-day notes grew patterns of responses to running, and from the patterns emerged the programs contained in this book.

From some 10,000 days of writing in a diary, I've learned which facts mean the most and how to review them. The essential information can fit onto one sheet of paper per month, divided into these columns:

- *Day of the month.* Keep a daily record, even if you don't run every day.
- *Amount of running.* Note the total time.
- *Amount of racing or testing.* Count only the part run significantly longer or faster than normal.
- *Notes.* Indicate extraordinary experiences, either good or bad: personal records, injuries, etc.

Most runners keep weekly records. This is too short a period to give an accurate reading of what you have accomplished. I prefer a monthly accounting (see the sample month in Table A). At month's end, add up the total running time for the month and divide by the total number of days (even if you have taken days off). This calculation yields the average daily length of your runs, which should fall in the thirty- to sixty-minute range.

Next, record the distances and times of the month's races and tests. Add up your amount of racing and testing for the month, and divide that figure into the total amount of running for the month. This gives the percentage of race-like effort, which should not exceed ten percent.

Finally, as you review the month's notes, look for connections between the numbers and your physical highs and lows. Then try to duplicate the conditions that led to the ups while eliminating the factors that produced the downs.

Table A A Month's Records

Month/Day	Run Time	Race/Test Distance	Race/Test Time	Race/Test Pace (mile)
4/1	30 minutes			
4/2	45 minutes			
4/3	45 minutes			
4/4	31 minutes			
4/5	36 minutes			

Table A—Continued

Month/Day	Run Time	Race/Test Distance	Race/Test Time	Race/Test Pace (mile)
4/6	40 minutes			
4/7	45 minutes	5-K	20:10	6:30
4/8	45 minutes			
4/9	47 minutes			
4/10	45 minutes			
4/11	30 minutes			
4/12	32 minutes			
4/13	45 minutes			
4/14	55 minutes	10-K	39:25	6:21
4/15	30 minutes			
4/16	32 minutes			
4/17	30 minutes			
4/18	15 minutes			
4/19	30 minutes			
4/20	17 minutes			
4/21	15 minutes			
4/22	30 minutes			
4/23	20 minutes			
4/24	30 minutes			

Table A—Continued

Month/Day	Run Time	Race/Test Distance	Race/Test Time	Race/Test Pace (mile)
4/25	15 minutes			
4/26	15 minutes			
4/27	21 minutes			
4/28	17 minutes			
4/29	20 minutes			
4/30	30 minutes			

- Days of running: 30 of 30
- Total running time: 930 minutes
- Average daily running time: 31 minutes
- Range of running times: 15 to 55 minutes
- Racing or testing days: 2 of 30
- Total racing/testing time: 59:35
- Range of racing/testing distances: 5 to 10 kilometers
- Range of racing paces: 6:21 to 6:30 per mile
- Percentage of racing/testing time: 6.4%
- Notes: Made the mistake of racing when a cold was developing, and it restricted running for the last half of the month.

Order the computerized edition of *Running Your Best Race*

Wm. C. Brown Publishers presents a new kind of sports book . . .

You can order a ready to run diskette for your Apple II series computer or IBM PC. The program diskette goes further than the book by allowing you to have an automated and personalized running program that plans, calculates, records, reviews, and updates your running program in no more time than it takes to select from the Menu of Programs and key in basic information about yourself.

The programs are advanced tools that go beyond the book to tailor Joe Henderson's advice to your needs in the areas of planning, pace, distance, running frequency, and training.

Apple II Series Version ISBN 0–697–00705–7

IBM PC Version ISBN 0–697–00727–8

Running Requirements: 48K and 1 disk drive

	Quantity	Title/Order #	Price
Name _____	_____	_____	_____
Address _____	_____	_____	_____
City _____		Amount of order	$ _____
State _____ Zip _____		Tax (CA, IA, LA residents add sales tax)	$ _____
Please indicate method of payment.		Shipping & handling ($1.00 per selection)	$ _____
☐ Check/money order enclosed (WCB pays shipping and handling)			
☐ Charge my credit account ☐ Visa ☐ Mastercard ☐ American Express		**Total**	$ _____

Account No.   MC Bank #

☐☐☐☐☐☐☐☐☐☐☐☐☐☐☐☐   ☐☐☐☐

Exp. Date _____ Signature _____
                                    Required of all Charges

wcb
Wm. C. Brown Publishers
2460 Kerper Blvd. / P.O. Box 539 / Dubuque, Iowa 52001